SATYAJIT RAY

TRAVAILS WITH THE ALIEN

THE FILM THAT WAS NEVER MADE AND OTHER ADVENTURES WITH SCIENCE FICTION

TRAVAILS WITH
THE ALIEN

THE FILM THAT WAS NEVER MADE AND
OTHER ADVENTURES WITH SCIENCE FICTION

TRAVAILS WITH
THE ALIEN

THE FILM THAT WAS NEVER MADE AND
OTHER ADVENTURES WITH SCIENCE FICTION

SATYAJIT RAY

EDITED BY **SANDIP RAY**

IN ASSOCIATION WITH
DHRITIMAN CHATERJI, ARUP K. DE, RIDDHI GOSWAMI & DEEPAK MUKERJEE

Harper
Collins

Society for the Preservation of
Satyajit Ray Archives

First published in India by
HarperCollins *Publishers* in 2018
A-75, Sector 57, Noida, Uttar Pradesh 201301, India
www.harpercollins.co.in

In association with
SOCIETY FOR THE PRESERVATION OF SATYAJIT RAY ARCHIVES

2 4 6 8 10 9 7 5 3 1

P-ISBN: 978-93-5277-915-4
E-ISBN: 978-93-5277-916-1

Cover design and book layout by PINAKI DE

Typeset in Adobe Caslon Pro by Pinaki De

Printed and bound at
Thomson Press (India) Ltd

To Bijoya Ray

CONTENTS

FOREWORD

Sandip Ray having a look at one of the 8mm sci-fi films collected by his father

"A science fiction addict"—that's the phrase Satyajit Ray, my father, used to describe his love for science fiction. As a schoolboy he was deeply fascinated by the stories of Jules Verne and H.G. Wells, which germinated his interest in this particular genre. In 1961, he along with his poet-friend Subhash Mukhopadhyay revived the children's magazine *Sandesh*, founded in 1913 by my great-grandfather Upendrakishore Ray Chowdhury. With the urge to feed *Sandesh*, his childhood love found a creative outlet as stories using all kinds of staple science fiction themes. Thus emerged the scientist-inventor character of Professor Shonku, which became an extremely popular series among young and old alike.

Along with his writings, Father was actively involved with the Bengali science fiction magazine *Aschorjo* as its chief patron, and later became the president of the Science Fiction Cine Club—probably the first one of its kind in India as well as abroad. I have fond memories of attending the film screenings of the club, accompanying him on several occasions. In my childhood days, local offices of all the major studios had a 16mm film library. My father used to select movies from these collections for screening on my birthdays—a memorable attraction for me and my friends. I can recall one such viewing of *Gorgo*—the British monster movie directed by Eugène Lourié. In those pre-video days we also had 8mm home movie collections available for sale. We had an 8mm projector in our house and Father used to bring condensed versions of sci-fi films every time he went abroad. This is how we saw *It Came from Outer Space*, the old version of *One Million BC*, starring Victor Mature, and a lot of other films. As an avid reader of science fiction, he immensely enjoyed the works of Arthur C. Clarke, Ray Bradbury, Isaac Asimov, Theodore Sturgeon and John Wyndham—*The Midwich Cuckoos* being one of his personal favourites. He subscribed to *Omni* and *Heavy Metal* magazines and hunted pavement stalls for interesting issues of *Science Digest*. He had a keen interest in science fiction writings bordering on the supernatural and paranormal, and always had an open mind about it.

"Bonkubabur Bandhu" ("Bonkubabu's Friend")—a short story by Father first published in *Sandesh*—served as a springboard for the script of his proposed science fiction film *The Alien*. The script was taken up by Columbia Pictures in Hollywood, with initial casting in progress, but a fateful turn of events under queer circumstances finally led to abandoning the project. The present volume is an in-depth documentation of the background of this much talked-about unmade film and offers an insight into Ray's creative oeuvre in the realm of science fiction. Though many know about the ill-fate of *The Alien*, this is the first time the making has been exhaustively collated with the unseen storyboard, stills, interviews, news reports and letters which make this book a unique piece of movie-making history.

SANDIP RAY

Member Secretary
Society for the Preservation of Satyajit Ray Archives,
Kolkata

THOUGHTS ON
SCIENCE
FICTION

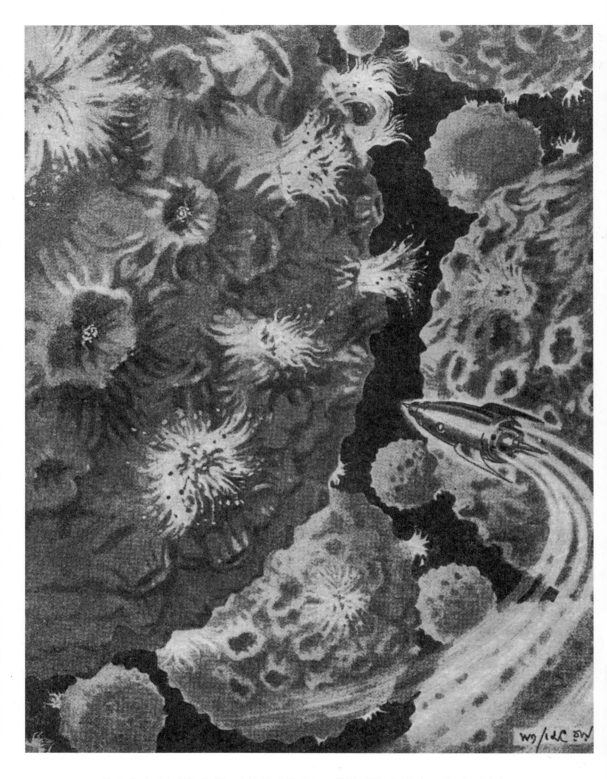

Illustration by Satyajit Ray for "Byomjatrir Diary" ("An Astronaut's Diary"), the first Professor Shonku adventure. The illustration was first published in *Sandesh*, December 1961

SF

SATYAJIT RAY

Now MAGAZINE, 21 OCTOBER 1966

Heaven knows the initials are not as widely familiar as one would wish. But to the true aficionado, that sibilant and that fricative are the hiss and swish of the rocket that take him to the farthest reaches of man's fancy, into the blackness of outer void, beyond the galaxies and beyond solar systems yet to be perceived and christened.

In his survey of science fiction, *New Maps of Hell*, Kingsley Amis observes that addiction to the genre occurs either at adolescence or not at all. I have a feeling he is right, because I am yet to meet an adult addict who didn't say he had "been reading the stuff for a very long time".

In my own case, it happened around the age of ten, when my granduncle Kuladaranjan Ray's splendid translation of Jules Verne's *Mysterious Island* came out in two yellow volumes. I was enthralled then as I am now by Verne's power to grip and persuade by sheer abundance of convincing detail. Verne was, of course, the pioneer, but not the sort of pioneer that makes tentative advances into a new territory and leaves it to posterity to do the exploring. He was prodigiously gifted with a speculative imagination. On top of that he was both industrious and thorough. He wrote his first fantasy *Five Weeks in a Balloon* at the age

Book cover of Kuladaranjan Ray's translation of Jules Verne's *Mysterious Island*. Cover design by Satyajit Ray

Headpiece illustration by Satyajit Ray for Kuladaranjan
Ray's translation of *Mysterious Island* in *Sandesh*

of thirty-five. From then on he produced one or two such novels every year for something like thirty years. And in all these years, while there were indifferent works interspersed between striking and important ones, Verne never repeated himself thematically.

Verne realized early the pitfalls of the new genre; for instance, you couldn't afford to let the fantasy soar, like a fairy tale, on a plane of pure make-believe. It had to have trappings of reality, and all the manner of pains had to be taken so that the reality didn't find itself adrift in a sea of speculation. One of the devices Verne used was to make the characters part of a carefully recreated historical event, and weave that event into the fabric of the fantasy. Thus the American Civil War triggers off an escape in a balloon which lands its occupants in the mysterious island. The Sepoy Mutiny and Nana Sahib are very much part of *Tigers and Traitors*, a fantasy laid in India. *Around the World in Eighty Days*, though not a science fantasy, is nevertheless a pretty tall story which encircles the globe and colours every episode in every country with touches of authentic local details. The episode in India is particularly rich in information on the then newly opened railways.

Verne read H.G. Wells and spoke disparagingly of his improbable flights of fancy. Reading Wells today, one sees the points of Verne's objection. Wells's approach to science fiction was poetic and romantic, and he had all the romantic poetic aversion to cold facts. How does the invisible man become invisible? We don't know because the three fat leather-bound notebooks which hold his secret are with the landlord of "that little inn in Port Stowe", and he will neither part with them nor disclose their contents. This is how Griffin, the Invisible Man himself, describes the process to his physician friend:

> I will tell you Kemp, sooner or later, all the complicated processes. We need not go into that now ... but the essential phase was to place the transparent object whose refractive index was to be lowered, between two radiating centres of a sort of ethereal vibration, of which I will tell you more fully later ... I wanted two little dynamos, and these I worked with a cheap gas engine. My first experiment was with a wool fabric...

TIME MACHINE

There are two typical Wells elements in this: a dash of scientific patter, and a modus operandi that is made to sound absurdly simple, and yet is wholly never described. Take *The Time Machine*. Here even the scientific patter has been dispensed with, save for a brief reference by the Time Traveller to the theoretical possibilities of travelling in the 4th Dimension. The machine is thus described:

> The thing that the Time Traveller held in his hand was a glittering metallic framework, scarcely larger than a small clock, and very delicately made. There was ivory in it, and a transparent crystalline substance…
>
> "This little affair," said the Time Traveller, resting his elbow on the table and pressing the hands together above the apparatus, "is only a model. It is my plan for a machine to travel through time. You will notice that it looks singularly askew, and there is an odd twinkling appearance about this bar, as though it was in some way unreal … also, here is one little white lever, and here is another."

One lever for the past and one for the future—what could be simpler? Although a scientist, Wells chose, in his science fiction, to skirt technology and concentrate on fiction. What really fascinated is not the breakthrough itself, but its aftermath. This gave Wells a freedom and flexibility which Verne never had. Verne devoted twenty-six chapters out of a total of twenty-eight of *From the Earth to the Moon* to describing and making of the projectile that was to make the first lunar trip. Although his mode of moon travel will hardly do for our time, the story at least proves that his main concern was technology. Throughout his career he kept stressing this aspect, prognosticating on its basis and coming up with inventions that confront man with new sensations, new experiences, new adventures. If his science now appears perfunctory, his prescience does not, for he was able to foresee, among other things, the submarine, the helicopter, television, motion picture and space flight.

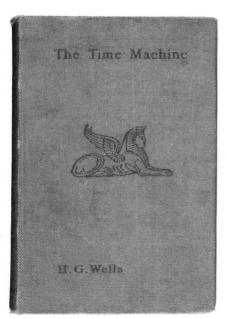

The first UK edition of *The Time Machine*
(Publisher: William Heinemann, 1895)

Today we grant both Verne and Wells honourable places in the hierarchy of science fiction writers. Apart from being pioneers, they are the progenitors of the two main types of science fiction as it exists today. We may roughly term them as prosaic and poetic. The first uses available scientific data as a springboard, but never lets the imagination soar beyond the limits of probability. The second gives freer rein to fancy, either ignores or circumvents facts, and tries to build conviction on a poetic plane. Of course, there are numerous stories where these two overlap, and some of the best modern science fiction is being written by scientists like Arthur Clarke and Isaac Asimov who achieve fine prophetic flights of fancy without losing their grip on scientific postulates.

In this era of rapidly developing technology, science fiction is inevitably undergoing transformations. The old staples are being replaced by new ones, and the field is being constantly enriched by new breakthroughs in every branch of applied science. The laser beam, computer machines, space satellites, androids (which are robots in human forms), suspended animation—these are among common ingredients of contemporary science-fiction. The moon is now nearly out as a field of speculation. Invisibility and time travel have been proved scientifically unattainable, and have lost their status as staples. Robots are having a field day, but malevolent ones are frowned upon, as hostility is regarded as a psychological state which a machine is incapable of attaining. ESP or extrasensory perception is coming into its own, thanks to recent findings, and extraterrestrials are being freely endowed with the powers of hypnosis and telepathy.

For the poets, the most fertile field would be the extraterrestrial, to which lack of knowledge imparts the nebulousness necessary for the poetic imagination to work upon. Even Mars, the nearest planet, remains clouded, both literally and metaphorically. But of course, the SF writer hardly restricts himself to our solar system. The field today is virtually limitless.

But any story of human endeavour on a familiar terrestrial plane has to have the backing of scientific data. Rockets may soar into space but if they set out from the earth, and if they contain human beings, there is no other way to but treat the happenings in a factual, scientific way.

But this is not necessarily an inhibiting factor. For one thing, the imponderables of human behaviour are always there to set off against the cold predictability (barring accidents) of machines. For another, for the vast mass of lay readers, technology still has enough elements of fantasy in it. As long as a man himself has not sensed weightlessness, or felt the searing upthrust of the rocket or fathomed a fraction of the infinite complexities of a giant computer, for him the elements of wonder will persist in clinging to the very ideas.

It is this sense of wonder that science fiction thrives on, and will continue to do so as long as there are men willing to dip into a tale that will make him feel small in the face of the expanding universe, and let him share the triumph and the futility of men probing into spheres of darkness—in space, on earth, on an alien planet, or in his own mind and body.

A LOOK AT
SCIENCE FICTION FILMS

SATYAJIT RAY

AMRITA BAZAR PATRIKA, PUJA ANNUAL, 1966

S CIENCE FICTION and espionage stories are said to be gradually displacing the thriller and the whodunit from their position of eminence in the field of light reading. I don't know what has caused the Spy-Boom—probably James Bond—but science fiction was bound to come into its own in an era of rapid technological advance, when even the layman's imagination is being tickled by close-up photos of the surface of the moon, and of astronauts floating weightlessly in space.

In itself, science fiction is not a new thing. In the form in which we know it today, it has existed for at least a century, ever since Jules Verne wrote *Five Weeks in a Balloon*. Verne remained a lone practitioner until H.G. Wells came out with *The Time Machine* and followed it up with a dozen or so of his celebrated imaginary adventures.

By the end of the first decade of the present century, the new genre may be said to have taken roots, and ever since then, it has continued to be enriched sporadically. The present state of luxurious growth is a post–World War II phenomenon, with USA, Britain, France, Soviet Russia and Czechoslovakia, all contributing to the mainstream.

Cinema has reflected a similar growth in science fiction ever since George Melies of France made *A Trip to the Moon* and other similar fantasies way back in the primitive days of the silent cinema.

Melies was primarily out to entertain his simple audience with "special effects". This is not surprising, since the illusionist possibilities of the motion picture was bound to strike the more inventive and frolicsome of the pioneers. And we should remember that Melies was a fellow countryman of Verne.

The iconic image from *A Trip to the Moon*

But Melies's scale was small, as it had to be in those days. The big fantasies had to wait until the 1920s when Germany came out triumphantly with Fritz Lang's ambitious *Metropolis*. This was a futurist fantasy which triumphed by virtue of its designing and

Metropolis poster, 1927

execution: No one excelled the Germans in craftsmanship in those days. The subject of the film was the human situation in a world dominated by machines. This had been a favourite theme of the science fiction writers, and H.G. Wells himself was to write a similar prophetic story called *The Shape of Things to Come*. This was filmed by Alexander Korda and was the biggest film to have come out of a British Studio in the '30s.

Both *Metropolis* and *The Shape of Things to Come* set out to stun the imagination with spectacle. Of course, they had their social messages too. But since they looked several centuries ahead, the contemporary viewer felt little emotional involvement with the issues. In other words, they were cold looks into the future.

This particular preoccupation is not very much in vogue these days—at least not in films. Now there are new themes and new categories—so many of them, in fact, that it is no longer possible to lump together all science fiction films, as it was even twenty years ago.

For instance, there is one category—rather low in the scale—which deals with "monsters", which are usually known or unknown species of prehistoric animals which may emerge from the depths of the ocean, or be freed by some explosion, atomic or otherwise, from a state of refrigeration somewhere in the polar regions.

Another category, slightly higher up, takes ordinary, harmless, creatures like ants or flies or spiders, and has them undergo mutation of monstrous proportions through some accident of science or nature.

A third category pits man against the forces of alien planets. This one has subdivisions, because you can have man going out to other planets, or you can have aliens descending on earth. You can even have an alien exerting influence by remote control, so that man is faced with the menace in a disembodied form, so to say.

The fourth and the last category finds man menaced by his own technology. This is, of course, the classical Frankenstein situation, but the variations it has brought forth are numerous. The Robot, which takes the place of the monster in the Frankenstein story, has been featured both wittily and terrifyingly in a number of science fiction films, the best of which is perhaps *Forbidden Planet*. But Robot is not the only manmade thing that provides a source of peril. Even Giant Computer Machines ("Giant Brains"—as they are called) have been pictured as developing a will of their own and turning against their creators.

These categories have existed almost ever since science fiction attained sophistication, around the early '40s. But this genre of films has never been widely popular, except when done on a big scale with considerable fanfare—as with *War of the Worlds*, *Forbidden Planet* and Disney's *Twenty Thousand Leagues under the Sea*. Modest, imaginative films have been made alongside these, but their very scale has suggested that the makers had been aware of the risks involved.

It seems, however, that a time has come at last when science fiction films will be looked upon as no bigger risks than, say, a "thriller". Not only that, the genre has started attracting directors who could hardly be associated with frivolous pursuits. Truffaut and Godard in France, Joseph Losey and Stanley Kubrick in the USA are either making or have already made their first science fiction films. Kubrick's film, called *2001: A Space Odyssey*, is being shot in a British studio. I was able to watch a day's work on it last July in the company of Arthur Clarke, astronomer, Kalinga Prize–winner and science fiction writer, who is the co-author of *A Space Odyssey* with Kubrick.

The amount of research that has gone into the film is fantastic. Clarke has made sure that nothing goes into the film that is not scientifically accurate. Thousands of sketches, plans and diagrams of space suits, rockets, moon buses and satellite stations fill the shelves and drawers and strew the floors of the dozen or so offices of the MGM studio where the film is being shot. One large room is given over to models—of space ships, landing stations, and satellites. The systematic thoroughness of the whole undertaking has to be seen to be believed. Since the story involves a trip to the moon, a rocket constitutes one of its most important elements. I met the designer of the rocket. He turned out to be one of the top men in the field of actual rocket designing. In other words, the rocket used in the film was theoretically capable of making actual space flights, although it never had to leave the studio floor.

When I arrived on the set, a shot was being taken of the control panel of the rocket. For this purpose, sixteen 16mm cameras had been set up behind the control board and were simultaneously projecting sixteen animated charts in colour to sixteen viewing panels on the board. And these are the panels which the 70mm camera was photographing. Clarke said that all those charts would make sense to a scientist.

Both the meticulousness and the scale seemed to uphold the claim of the makers of *A Space Odyssey*: That this was going to be the biggest film ever made. And biggest naturally also means the costliest.

As I left the studio that evening, I really had the feeling that science fiction was coming into its own at last; and that whatever else the future may hold for mankind, it certainly holds the promise of better and more serious science fiction films.

KUBRICK, TRUFFAUT AND SF

SATYAJIT RAY

ASCHORJO MAGAZINE, OCTOBER–NOVEMBER 1966

It is not very well known that films based on fantasy or science have been made since the early days of cinema. About sixty-five years ago, Georges Melies made *A Trip to the Moon* in France. It was a genuine fantasy film though satiric in mood. Since then, a large number of science fiction and fantasy films have been made abroad. I still remember *The Shape of Things to Come*, a film based on an H.G. Wells story, which was produced in 1932–33 in Britain by Alexander Korda.

Such films have been steadily made in Hollywood since *Dr. Jekyll & Mr. Hyde* released in 1922. It may not be wrong to say that there are some directors who have acquired special expertise in this particular genre. But those generally regarded as among the finest film-makers of the world have not tried their hands at this kind of films, until recently. Last year, the best film award at the Berlin Film Festival went to Jean-Luc Godard's *Alphaville*. No other science fiction film had ever received such an honour before. It is to the credit of the director of *Alphaville* that he presented a Paris of the future ruled by science by shooting his film not on artificial sets but in the streets, hotels, offices and other everyday places of today's city of Paris and through a clever use of light and camera angles. I have no hesitation in saying that it is an unforgettable film for its technical excellence.

We are familiar with the extraordinary talents of Francois Truffaut of France and Stanley Kubrick of the US through the French and American films they have made, respectively. Recently, they shot two films based on stories by two well-known science fiction writers on the floors of London's Elstree Studios. The floors stood almost next to each other. Truffaut based his film on Ray Bradbury's *Fahrenheit 451*. It was at his request and with his cooperation that Kubrick made his film, *2001: A Space Odyssey*, from an Arthur C. Clarke story.

Thanks to the intervention of Arthur C. Clarke, I got an opportunity to visit Elstree Studios during my recent trip to London. I was told that Truffaut had finished his shoot but Kubrick was still working on his film. I was amazed to see the sets of the inside of a spaceship on the floor. I spoke to Kubrick for a couple of minutes and then struck up a conversation with the man who had planned the interiors of the rocket. I was surprised to learn that he was one of the world's best rocket designers. A prototype of the rocket he had designed had already been lifted into space. I asked him why he was working for films. Smiling, he said he earned more working for films than designing real rockets.

The makers of *2001: A Space Odyssey* claimed that such a big science fiction film had never been made before, and that no other producer would dare make a film about space in the next ten years. Witnessing the enthusiasm of Kubrick and his colleagues and the scale they worked on, this could well be true and justified.

Translated from the Bengali by **Arup K. De**

ALL INDIA RADIO INTERVIEW ON SF

AIR INTERVIEW WITH SATYAJIT RAY, 1982

PROLOGUE

A lifelong aficionado of science fiction, Satyajit Ray's deep and abiding interest in this genre is evident from his novels, short stories and articles. Ray was president of the Sci-Fi Cine Club set up in 1966—the first of its kind in the world. He also played a major role in selecting the films for the club's film shows. In 1961, Ray created the unique scientist-inventor character of Professor Shonku, who, in Ray's words, "may be said to be a mild-mannered version of Professor Challenger, where the love of adventure takes him to remote corners of the globe". Through his writings, Ray tried to inculcate a sense of wonder and imagination in the young reader's mind. His science fiction works often dwelled upon the fantastic and the supernatural, for which he had a special fascination. He once remarked, "Some of the stories I have written reflect my love of Verne and Wells and Conan Doyle, whose works I read as a schoolboy." But the quantum of enthusiasm and discussion on Ray's science fiction is regrettably meagre when compared to his detective fiction and films. That is why this interview on science fiction by All India Radio Kolkata is a valuable document. Recorded in 1982, Ray expressed his views openly on many aspects in a rare and candid conversation with noted science fiction author Sankarshan Roy, and psychologist Dr Amit Chakraborty. We have tried to capture the spirit of this discussion as closely as possible in this English translation.

SANKARSHAN: Science in literature, or science-based literature, has been a topic of discussion for quite some time, and science fiction is nowadays practised seriously by many. But I feel that literature, if it is not scientific, is not fruitful. What is your take on that?

SATYAJIT: Well, yes, one would think so. Science fiction or science fantasy, whatever you call it, is a separate genre of writing altogether. But when you are writing about human beings too, you delve into the science of psychology, which is often reflected in my films. In my films, my stories, you will always find a human psychological interplay. We always try to reach for that inner truth, be it in their relationships, or behaviour...

SANKARSHAN: Truth should always be scientific.

SATYAJIT: Whatever is written about the everyday experience of human life, or about foreign lands, or cities, or village life, or writing about people from different social strata—in all of these, you will find an inherent scientific approach. As I said, psychology is always present as a dominant factor, even if you are not well read on it as a science subject. But a writer must have that ability to find the truth through his observations.

AMIT: This power of observation that you mentioned—even that is a scientific method, isn't it?

SATYAJIT: Yes, it is.

AMIT: It has its own science in it.

SATYAJIT: It does, but we are not always aware of it. One possibly cannot label it as a separate science and write a book on it—although even that happens sometimes with language—language has its own science. The difference in the conversations of people from various social classes, milieu, situations; everything now falls within the domain of linguistics. For that matter, any element of your story can be linked to one scientific aspect, and if you are faithful in your approach towards it, that shows your scientific temper.

AMIT: So, can it be said that all writers should possess that scientific temper? Or that they should be scientifically aware of the global phenomena taking place in everyday life? Otherwise, it seems that even the works of writers who are not writing science fiction would not be fruitful enough.

SATYAJIT: Well, that can be said, more or less. But that does not mean you should be up-to-date about all the latest scientific experiments or inventions. That much is not required, and if you follow the trend today, the research periphery of different sciences— be it astronomy, or biology, or microbiology—is expanding. They are discussed in such depth that it is not possible for any writer to be well-informed about it.

AMIT: Let alone writers, it is even very difficult for a scientist of one specific field to be aware of the current research in another scientific domain.

SATYAJIT: Extremely difficult.

AMIT: It is becoming so diverse.

Satyajit: Tremendously diverse.

Amit: One can say in a general sense that we should have that scientific awareness, and one cannot possibly survive without it.

Satyajit: One is aware of these things, even if only from newspapers; one need not read voluminous science textbooks or the latest journals for that. So, the general learned people, or those whom we refer to as writers, should be aware—many already are—and those who are not, their creations will surely be enriched by the knowledge.

Amit: A little while ago, you mentioned both science fiction and science fantasy as scientific writings. But sometimes these are referred to as different genres, aren't they? Can you elaborate on that?

Satyajit: Well, there is a certain kind of story … let me give one example. If one has to write a story about a man taking a voyage to the moon, like Jules Verne had written long ago in *Journey to the Moon*, about voyages to the moon or other planets—I can especially recall the film *2001: A Space Odyssey*—these should have scientific details that are technically valid and correct in the eyes of even a scientist. As everybody knows what is humanly possible and impossible in science, one has to be well-read, thorough and technically flawless about the scientific details in them. But there is another type of story, which I had written once and planned to make a film out of, but it fell through eventually. Anyway, I had written a screenplay called *The Alien*, where the plot is about an alien creature from outer space coming to Earth. Now, the science and technology shown in this kind of spaceship is something beyond our knowledge, and there I had to depend on imagination to a large extent. There it is impossible for anybody to validate the scientific details, because one doesn't really know what's possible for them and what's not! Their planet is technologically far superior to us, and so we don't have a clue about their achievements and possibilities. So, there we can depend a lot on our imagination. There you can dwell on the realm of philosophy, or on the world of poetry. But when one is showing a man doing some kind of activity—even if it is fifty years down the line—one has to describe the setting while always keeping in mind the present state of technology.

Amit: I remember reading one of Mr Ray's articles some time ago about science fiction or science fantasy. Writing about H.G. Wells, you mentioned that he had described the time machine in an absurdly simple manner—push the button, and you're there. But even in *The Alien* project that you just mentioned, surely one has to retain some relevant scientific details to establish it in a believable manner.

Satyajit: Yes, obviously, because there cannot be anything without the remotest connection to Earth. It is difficult to imagine such a creature or a planet. If you study the origin of life at the very basic level of amino acids and other things, it seems to be identical everywhere, primarily all over Earth; and till now it is hypothesized that even if there is extraplanetary life somewhere, the fundamental elements of life would possibly be the same.

SANKARSHAN: I would state another related aspect here. We have also seen in many cases that the author's imagination has surpassed the scientist's imagination. Jules Verne's imagination at that time was not matched by any scientist. I have a feeling that in many cases scientists have followed science fiction writers, haven't they?

SATYAJIT: They have. Now, it is a fact that most of the great names of science fiction are also scientists themselves. Take, for example, Arthur C. Clarke. Clarke had written about satellites thirty years ago, long before today's age of INSAT satellites.

AMIT: One can also say the same about Asimov and others. They wrote about the dropping of the atom bomb in 1940, when nobody knew about the Manhattan Project. They brought out these ideas in their stories. One can find such concepts in contemporary science fiction magazines.

SATYAJIT: Definitely. For that matter, if you go back five hundred years or so, you will find Leonardo da Vinci doing what not! He had shown so many futuristic things during a period that can be called the formative years of science. A whole lot of things like the aeroplane, helicopter, gramophone, etc., came into his imagination. So, you see, human imagination is unbound, and although the science lags behind, it gradually tries to catch up if there is the slightest technological possibility within it, and one day it becomes a reality.

SANKARSHAN: There are similar stories about the Puranas.

SATYAJIT: Oh, yes. I have heard one such anecdote, probably true, regarding our shastras. Some Sanskrit scriptures on warfare were found in Hitler's war office. Germany always had a lot of Indologists and Sanskrit scholars, and one hears that the idea of a missile actually germinated from these! (*laughs*)

SANKARSHAN: Now, we would like to discuss your literary creations. You have been writing these science fiction stories and novels for quite some time now. How did you start writing them?

AMIT: If I may add, we have seen Premendra Mitra and a few others writing science fiction stories in Bengal in the 1920s and 1930s. But a scientist character like Professor Shonku was the first of its kind in the 1960s. We would like to know how you introduced such a unique character.

SATYAJIT: To be honest, I had no literary bent at all, and never thought I might one day write stories. I was working for an advertising agency, then left the job and started my film-making career. Then one day my poet-friend Subhash Mukhopadhyay suggested the idea of reviving our family magazine, *Sandesh*. The idea struck me and within six months, we brought out *Sandesh* with a new look, in 1961. Subhash and I were joint editors. With the publishing of *Sandesh*, naturally I thought of writing something, primarily to feed *Sandesh*. My very first story, "Bonkubabur Bandhu", can be said to be science fiction, but it was not a Professor Shonku story. This was my first Bengali story,* and it was this story that served as the basis for the science fiction film I had once planned. Anyway, after "Bonkubabur Bandhu", I wrote some ghost stories and a couple of other stories, and then I thought of creating a character like Professor Shonku. I had in mind the diary form of writing, and perhaps there was a subconscious influence of "Heshoram Hoshiar's Diary", my father's story, which I like immensely. This was a parody of Conan Doyle's *The Lost World*, where he created some absurd prehistoric creatures with weird names and habits, who have absolutely no resemblance with the real world.

Amit: The whole idea was to make fun.

Satyajit: Completely to make fun, to mock and pull some legs. It was a take-off on *The Lost World*, shall we say. My first Shonku story, "Byomjatrir Diary", also reflects that mood. On the surface, Shonku may appear to be a serious person, he keeps a diary, but his first invention, Nasyastra, a snuff gun, makes one sneeze fifty-six times non-stop (*laughs*),

Professor Shonku with his first invention—a snuff gun

and things like that. But gradually, Shonku became serious. He became serious because after this story, I avidly started reading science books, magazines and journals. Then it became a passion, reading voraciously the works of famous science fiction authors like

---

*Although Ray mentions "Bonkubabur Bandhu" as his first Bengali story, it is to be noted that his first published Bengali story is "Byomjatrir Diary" ("An Astronaut's Diary") in *Sandesh*, October to December, 1961. "Bonkubabur Bandhu" was originally published in *Sandesh*, February 1962.

Asimov, Arthur C. Clarke, Bradbury, Theodore Sturgeon, and others. And there are certain major themes that every science fiction author has used some time or the other. It may be the concept of longevity, invisibility, the brain, an alien coming from the outside, or man undertaking a space mission—these may be said to be the staples of science fiction, and I started using them one after another through Shonku. Also, we have a tremendous

Headpiece of "Byomjatrir Diary" in *Sandesh*, illustrated by Ray

fascination with some locations—Egypt, some areas of Africa, deserts, some ancient civilizations—many of which still puzzle us with unsolved mysteries. Take, for example, the building of pyramids itself—so unique a concept. I have a special attraction towards these ancient civilizations, things which are still mysterious to the modern world.

Amit: There are many things unsolved by present knowledge.

Satyajit: Many, many things. Still many more are gradually cropping up. I have recently written about one in *Sandesh*, about the Nazca Lines—I don't know if you know about it. There is a small region called Nazca in Peru. About forty years ago, a plane flying over it discovered incredibly spread-out geometric designs on the land—birds, insects, spiders, so huge that you cannot interpret them from the ground level, but only from a certain elevation, at least five hundred to six hundred feet above…

Amit: This is mentioned in Däniken's book.

Satyajit: Däniken has mentioned it, and a scientist from *National Geographic* has been there for ten years, trying to fathom the reason behind these. Däniken has straightaway said that these were made for the aliens, to help them land on Earth, etc., etc. All of these ideas have gradually been incorporated into Shonku. Later, Shonku was joined by his friends and some other characters. In the beginning, Shonku operated mostly in and around Giridih, but when the Felu character made his appearance, I kept the Felu adventures within India, and Shonku had to travel all around the globe. (*laughs*)

Amit: I would like to point out one thing here. You were saying that Shonku is much more serious now. We are also getting certain things that were not there in your stories earlier, like a little detail of a laboratory and things like that…

Satyajit: Yes … yes.

Professor Shonku's encounter with the aliens in "Byomjatrir Diary"

Professor Shonku in his laboratory in "Byomjatrir Diary"

Illustration from "Byomjatrir Diary"

AMIT: These are occurring more frequently now. That means you are bringing in these details and making them more scientifically valid.

SATYAJIT: Yes, but now I have to study a lot more for that. In the beginning, when I started Shonku, I was not so well read. Then, I started subscribing to some magazines, I immediately purchased any good book that came my way, read them, and now it's not sufficient to have a single book on one subject. Within two to three years, new books are coming out, and it is progressing at a speed beyond imagination. So, I try my best to be at par with the current trend, and within this periphery if I find something relevant, I use them in Shonku. But in Shonku and in Feluda, too, I have used something which is said to be still at the stage of the paranormal, shall we say … be it parapsychology, or something else. I have tremendous curiosity in that area too.

AMIT: What is your own opinion on this?

SATYAJIT: My opinion is … I have an open mind regarding this. I believe that these types of things do happen. I have seen them, in my own family. I'm not an eyewitness, but as it happened with an extremely close family member, it's almost the same as being an eyewitness, and there is no reason to disbelieve it. I have a feeling that these will come under the purview of science within the next thirty to forty years. The reason is still unknown, but slowly, all of these will come under particle physics or some other branch of science.

Amit: We know that many scientists are working on it.

Satyajit: Extensive research is going on in many places, like Soviet Russia. There is this Kirlian photography...

Amit: We were discussing Professor Shonku. We now wish to change the topic to another aspect—the urge behind writing science fiction or science fantasy. Should more of such works be written? What is the necessity? As we see in modern times, science communication, or informing people about scientific truths, is a very big issue. This may be done by science fiction as well as by science fantasy. If you could say something on this particular aspect...

Sankarshan: The main objective is to develop scientific awareness in people's minds. Is that possible through science fiction? And to what extent?

Satyajit: I would say it is possible, because you see, if my stories were not admired by readers, I wouldn't have been enthusiastic about writing more.

Sankarshan: Have you ever heard that your writings have inspired someone to take up science?

Amit: I would like to add here that when Arthur C. Clarke came to India to receive the Kalinga Award, he commented that we haven't kept account of how many people have chosen science as a profession after reading science fiction. Do you think this is another dimension of science fiction?

Satyajit: At least I have started writing science fiction after reading them! (*laughs*) At least I have benefited from it. Since I received that inspiration and started writing, there is no reason why others too will not be inspired. That may not be expressed always through literature; they may take it up later as a career. If they are deeply motivated by it, why wouldn't they try and probe more into it? They will not know everything from my stories. If they develop a really keen interest, they will have to read up various extra things on the topic out of their own desire. Ultimately, they may take it up within their academic discipline. Textbooks may not seem so interesting to teenagers, they mostly get information first from storybooks. So, the story is a very important factor here. The plot plays a very big role; it shouldn't be too information-heavy. One shouldn't feel that I am writing the story to present information. The main subject is the story, its spirit.

Along with the story, readers get some additional inputs that increase their curiosity about certain aspects, which they may use in the future if they so wish.

Amit: Apart from that, most science fiction writers dwell on the subject of futurology, about what may happen in the unseen and unknown future. When there was no rocket, we read about it, or read about the atom bomb, and developed an idea. Similarly, when writers are talking about events in 2000 or 2020, we are developing a vision from these. Don't you think that it will help us in adjusting to the unknown future? A sort of preparation?

Satyajit: But we will not be there in that future! (*laughs*) The generation keeps on changing…

Amit: No, but your readers are mostly teenagers. One day they will become adults…

Satyajit: Oh yes, they will become adults.

Sankarshan: What has remained in their imagination may one day become reality as well.

Satyajit: It may, who knows? It is not surprising at all. But we don't think of ourselves as that influential. We don't have the scientific background of the really brilliant authors, like Asimov or Arthur C. Clarke. So, we have to depend more on the plot, imagination, and the drama of the story. Along with that, we have to read up a bit, and try to add something so that it does not seem too absurd or bizarre.

Ray's logo of *Fantastic*, a Bengali sci-fi magazine

Sankarshan: We now wish to discuss science-based films, as most of them are adapted from science fiction stories. These days, one sees a lot of foreign films in the theatres, and most of them are science-based films.

Amit: Mr Ray himself had mentioned once that he also had a plan for making a science fiction film. It may not have been so monumental or gorgeous like *Space Odyssey*, but I think he had something in mind. What are you thinking about it now?

Satyajit: Yes, it was planned fifteen years ago, in 1967. I wrote a screenplay called *The Alien*. In fact, I once went to London when Stanley Kubrick was shooting for *Space Odyssey*. There, I met Arthur C. Clarke. I already had in mind an idea for a screenplay about an alien coming from outer space, loosely based on "Bonkubabur Bandhu". I told Clarke about it and he encouraged me to write a screenplay. On my return to Calcutta,

I wrote the full scenario. I sent the screenplay to Hollywood, where Columbia Pictures had agreed to back it. But the person who was working as the mediator created some problems and the film was never made. But several hundred cyclostyled mimeographed copies of the screenplay were there in the Columbia office, and bits and pieces of many ideas have permeated into two films—one is *Close Encounters of the Third Kind*, and the other is a new film by Spielberg, called *E.T.: The Extra-terrestrial*. Now the situation is such that I cannot make my *Alien*. I will be charged with plagiarism if I do, but the reality is just the opposite!

Amit: We didn't know about this at all!

Sankarshan: Did you plan it as an English film?

Satyajit: No, it was meant to be a bilingual film. It was a purely Bengali setting. In the dead of night, a spaceship plunges into a lotus pond in a remote village in Bengal with a sole alien creature inside it. As soon as it descends, all the limp lotus stalks straighten up and open their petals at the same time. We understand that it is a benevolent force. The spaceship, as well as the alien, are somewhat damaged, but with the first rays of the sun falling through the porthole, the alien becomes active once again. The story unfolds as it emerges from the spaceship, sometimes during the night, and we see many reactions around it. Apart from the villagers, there is one journalist chap doing a village survey; his wife is also with him. She is doing research on the family planning of village women. There is one Marwari businessman; he is working with an American engineer to drill tubewells in search of water—this is a drought-ravaged area. The real drama begins when the villagers notice the golden spire-like conical top of the spaceship sticking out of the water. They take it for a submerged temple-top that has come up due to the blasting. The Marwari plans to draw out water from the pond and restore the temple, and so on. Only the Bengali journalist has a hunch about the real thing because he senses that something weird is happening. This creature is very frail-looking; at first sight, one mistakes it for a sickly, hunger-stricken child. The eyes are replaced by sockets, and they have different visions—X-ray, telescopic, microscopic—each with a different-coloured ray. He possesses such supernatural powers that he can even bring the dead to life! There is a scene in the burning ground where the eldest member of the village is dying ... there are many such funny moments, you see.

Ultimately, the journalist goes to the engineer and tells him what he suspects. The engineer does not believe his words. "Are you mad? Why will they come to this godforsaken place? There are so many big cities in the West, what the hell are they doing here?" But finally, when he too begins to suspect the truth, he tries to combat it with his gun. The alien had actually come to collect some specimens—a frog, a snake, some plants, some flowers, and a very poor boy called Haba. He is an orphan beggar boy. The alien has understood that he has no future here, so it is also taking him along. By the time the engineer arrives, the alien's spaceship is ready to leave. At the climax, the engineer fires his gun, but the spaceship takes off in a flash, leaving everybody bewildered. The villagers are under the impression that this foreigner has saved them from great danger, but the American himself knows that he hasn't done anything! (*laughs*)

SANKARSHAN: Why don't you make it now?

SATYAJIT: Now it is possible. Earlier, there were some technical difficulties, but now they have become extremely easy.

SANKARSHAN: Please make it.

SATYAJIT: Let's see. I have to make some changes, because these American films have lifted some ideas.

AMIT: Still, the way you described the story, it will be superb.

SATYAJIT: I have shown certain things through its eyes—say a leaf, or an insect— the microscopic vision gradually zooms into the insect and finally the whole screen is filled with its veins and arteries … its whole system … everything can be seen.

AMIT: It has ample scope from the filmic point of view too.

SATYAJIT: The interesting part is, the materialistic science shown here will be okay, but the inside of the spaceship does not have any panels or switches; the whole area has a feel of veins and arteries. As if this is also…

AMIT: A living being.

SATYAJIT: A living being, and you have to make certain changes to make it live. There is a life-like rhythmic glow all the time. This whole idea was thought out long ago, and even today there are attempts to revive it. Letters of request keep coming from America. But I had such a bitter experience, that I do not feel … if there is again some … Now one sees so many space fictions being filmed, and frankly speaking, they are technically outstanding.

SANKARSHAN: Couldn't you get the studio facilities from abroad? Surely you can!

SATYAJIT: Yes, of course. If I have to do it, it wouldn't be possible without co-production. I have to take money from abroad, because it is an expensive proposition. This creature—it has a peculiar gait, it hops and jumps from one place to another. It is so light that it can even stand on a leaf; it is almost weightless, one can say. One day, this American is returning from a tribal dance, he has had some country liquor. While coming through a bamboo grove, he is followed by the alien. He takes him for a famished child and throws a coin at him; and when the alien is going back, the coin is seen stuck on its forehead! (*laughs*)

Amit: Many thanks to Mr Ray. He has spared a lot of time for us today. We also thank Mr Sankarshan Roy. I think our listeners will have enjoyed today's discussion a lot.

Translated from the Bengali by **Riddhi Goswami**

Ray's illustration of "Byomjatrir Diary", first published in *Sandesh*, 1961

SCI-FI CINE CLUB DOCUMENTS

DESIGNED BY
SATYAJIT RAY, 1966

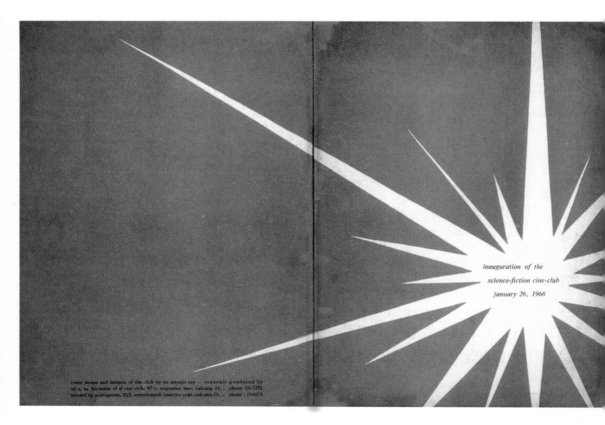

Spread of the brochure designed by Satyajit Ray on the inauguration of Sci-Fi Cine Club in 1966

inauguration of the science-fiction cine-club
january 26, 1966 / academy of fine arts

The insignia/logo of the club as printed (far right corner of the page) in the brochure was also created by Ray

objects of
sf cine club

To organise shows of science-
fiction and fantasy films and allied
performances exclusively for members.
To propagate, spread and further the
study of science-fiction and fantasy films.
To increase the appreciation of such
films for the common good of the society as a whole.
To help encouraging scientific imagination through
scientific films, and related symposiums and publications.
To influence the film industry as a whole for production of
science-fiction and fantasy films of desired standard
for the enlightenment of the society.

The objective of the club as mentioned in the brochure

they are the promoters

Name	Address	Occupation
Satyajit Ray *President*	3, Lake Temple Road Calcutta-29	Film Producer and Director
Premendra Mitra *Vice-President*	57, Harish Chatterjee Street Calcutta-26	Writer and Journalist
Ajit Karmakar *Treasurer*	14/1A, Suri Lane, Suite E, Calcutta-14	Service
Asim Bardhan *Member,* *Executive Committee*	97/1, Serpentine Lane, Calcutta-14	Educationist
Sukriti Mohan Bhowmic	Block 5, Flat 7, Govt. Housing Estate, Sodpur: 24-Parganas	Service
Sukhendu Das	25-A, Suri Lane, Calcutta-14	Business
R. P. Mukherjee	28-B, Suri Lane, Calcutta-14	Service
Srikanta Mitra	33/1, Suri Lane, Calcutta-14	Service
Manab Dutta	22, Mahatma Gandhi Road, Calcutta-9	Business
P. K. Banerjee	Rly. Qrs. No. T54D, Kaiser Street, Calcutta-9	Sportsman
Asoke Chatterjee	46/7, Mahatma Gandhi Road, Calcutta-9	Lawyer
Adrish Bardhan *Secretary*	97/1, Serpentine Lane, Calcutta-14	Writer and Journalist

The "promoters" of the club included Satyajit Ray and the well-known Bengali writer Premendra Mitra

Our Secretary Speaks (Extract)

Ladies and Gentlemen,

The idea to form a film society exclusively for science fiction and fantasy films was mooted by a few sf enthusiasts who also happen to be the contributors to India's first sf monthly magazine "Aschorjo" since its inception.

I was entrusted with the great honour and heavy responsibility of executing the idea and giving a shape to India's first Science Fiction Cine Club. We are proud to have India's two great sons as our President and Vice-President. It is well known that our President is not only an internationally famous film director but also a sf devotee and writer of excellent sf stories. And our Vice-President, Sri Premendra Mitra, is a pioneer in sf literature in India, inspiring many in the field including the present Secretary.

Our work has been much easier by the active co-operation and guidance of these two great sf devotees. Sri Satyajit Ray, busy as he is, managed to snatch some time for designing the symbol of the club which is entirely his creation. He also voluntarily did layouts for our membership card, etc. and cover design for the souvenir...

As to the role played by sf, i.e., science fiction, in the popularisation of science, Arthur C. Clarke says in his speech at UNESCO while receiving the Kalinga Prize in 1962:

"Though it often serves to impart information, I think its chief value is inspirational rather than educational."

I recall an incident which corroborates the above fact. In a get-together in New York a few young Bengalee Scientists admitted to our Vice-President, Sri Premendra Mitra, that his award-winning *Ghana da* stories had great influence on their careers.

This is no doubt a great achievement of sf literature in Bengal. We hope more and our long-cherished dream will come true when we will have the opportunity to screen India's first sf film classic produced in Calcutta by the daring genius Sri Satyajit Ray, our esteemed President. And along with him (or perhaps I should say being inspired by his work) will come a whole group of progressive film-makers who will dedicate their talents to the creation of new styles of their own in this new field...

ADRISH BARDHAN

feelings of our president

Having been a Science-fiction addict for close on thirty years, the idea of the formation of an sf cine club has an obvious appeal to me. I am happy to be associated with the club—which may very well be one of the first of its kind—here or abroad. On the occasion of the club's inauguration, may I wish its members many exciting and thought-provoking sessions of the best SF films from all over the world.

SATYAJIT RAY

"One is grateful for the presence of sf as a medium in which our society can criticise itself and sharply. '1984' and 'Farenheit 451' are such horribly drawn pictures of the hell."

—KINGSLEY AMIS.

"Our civilization is no more than the sum of all the dreams that earlier ages have brought to fulfilment. And so it must always be, for if man cease to dream, if they turn their backs upon the wonder of the Universe, the story of our race will come to an end."

—ARTHUR C. CLARKE.

The particular page of the brochure where Ray expresses his "feelings" about his association with the Club

They share the joy with us (selected quotes)

"I wish all the best to the newly formed SF Cine Club. I think anything we can do today to enlighten and bring culture into the lives of young folks is worthy of the fullest encouragement."—WALT DISNEY, Disneyland, California

"As one who has loved sf and fantasy films all his life, and been influenced by them in his writing of stories, I send you the heartiest of wishes as you come together to express your enthusiasm for this form, I gather you are not snobs. Thanks all the fates and circumstances for that. I wish you much fun and high times and good thinking about what you see. You will travel into the far future to see what we might one day be, but more important, through fantasy, examine our own deep present, and try to guess what we are in this strange hour. I envy you your beginnings. I relish with you the events immediately ahead."—RAY BRADBURY, Los Angeles, California

"I wish the club every success, and feel that it has been started at an auspicious time. Science fiction film-making has, it seems, suddenly come of age, with a number of serious productions by leading directors."—ARTHUR C. CLARKE, London

"Congratulations all around. You are helping to further one of the most thrilling— and most profound—forms of art in the modern world. I salute your imagination and resource."—KINGSLEY AMIS, Maida Vale

"It gives me the greatest pleasure to hear about such an excellent and interesting idea as the SF Cine Club, and I do wish you every success. I shall be thinking of you on the 26th January, and only wish that I could be in Calcutta on that occasion. I was in Triste as one of the guests of honour at the First International Science Fiction Film Festival in 1963; I am only sorry that Calcutta is too far away for me to reach."
— BRIAN ALDISS, Wheatley, Oxford

arthur c. clarke

on

the value of science-fiction

What role does science fiction actually play in the popularization of science? Though it often serves to impart information, I think its chief value is inspirational rather than educational. How many young people have had the wonders of the universe first opened up to them, or have been turned to a scientific career by the novels of the Verne and Wells? Many distinguished scientists have paid tribute to the influence of those great masters; and a careful survey would, I believe, reveal that science-fiction is a major factor in launching many youngsters on a scientific career.

In one field in particular—that of astronautics —the influence of science-fiction has been enormous. The four greatest pioneers of space flight —Tsiolkovsky, Oberth, Goddard & Von Braun all wrote sf to propagate their ideas (though they did not always get it published).

In spreading the ideas of spaceflight, sf has undoubtedly helped to change the world. More generally, it helps us to face the strange realities of the universe in which we live. This is well put in an article recently sent to me by a sf fan who also happens to be a Nobel Prize Winner, Dr. Muller: "The real world is increasingly seen to be, not the tidy little garden of our race's childhood, but the extraordinary, extravagant universe described by the eye of science ... If our art ... does not explore the relations and contingencies implicit in the greater world into which we

are forcing our way and does not reflect the hopes and fears based on these appraisals, then that art is a dead pretence ... But man will not live without art. In a scientific age, he will therefore have science fiction."

In the same paper, Dr. Muller points out another valuable service that this type of literature has performed. "Recent s.f." he writes, "must be accorded high credit for being one of the most active forces in support of equal opportunities, goodwill and co-operation among all human beings, regardless of their racial and rational origins. Its writers have been practically unanimous in their adherence to the ideal of 'one free world'.

That, I think, is inevitable. Anyone who reads this form of literature must quickly realise the absurdity of mankind's present tribal divisions. S.F. encourages the cosmic viewpoint; perhaps this is why it is not popular among those literary pundits who have never quite accepted the Copernican revolution, nor grown used to the idea that Man may not be highest form of life in the universe. The sooner such people complete their education, and re-orientate themselves to the astronomical realities, the better. And s.f. is one of the most effective tools for this urgent job.

For this is, pre-eminently, the literature of change and change is the only thing of which we can be certain today, thanks to the continuing

Extracts from the lecture delivered by Arthur C. Clarke at UNESCO on 27 September 1962 and accelerating Scientific Revolution. What we s.f. writers call "mainstream literature" usually paints a static picture of society, presenting, as it were, a snapshot of it, frozen at one moment in time. S.F., on the other hand, assumes that the future will be profoundly different from the past —though it does not, as is often imagined, attempt to predict that future in detail. Such a feat is impossible, and the occasional direct hits of Wells and other writers are the result of luck as much as judgment.

But by mapping out possible future, as well as a good many impossible ones, the s.f. writer can do a great service to the community. He encourages in his readers flexibility of mind, readiness to accept and even welcome change—in one word, adaptability. Perhaps no attribute is more important in this age. The dinosaurs disappeared because they could not adopt to their changing environment. We shall disappear if we cannot adopt to their changing environment. We shall disappear if we cannot adopt to an environment which now contains space ships and thermonuclear weapons.

Sir Charles Snow ends his famous essay "Science and Government" by stressing the vital importance of "the gift of foresight". He points out that men often have wisdom without possessing foresight. Perpahs we s.f. writers sometimes show foresight without wisdom; but at least we undoubtedly do have foresight, and it may rub off on to the community at large.

(Part of the address delivered at UNESCO by Arthur C. Clarke after receiving the Kalinga Prize on 27-9-62)

kingsley amis

on

definition of science-fiction & fantasy

With the 'fiction' part we are on reasonably secure ground. The 'science' part raises several kinds of difficulty one of which is that sf is not necessarily fiction about science or scientists nor is science necessarily important in it. sf is that kind of 'prose narrative' treating of a situation that could not arise in the world we know, but which is hypothesised on the basis of some innovation in science or technology, pseudoscience or pseudotechnology, whether human or extra terrestrial in origin.

Immediately adjacent to sf field, and in some instances to be distinguished from it only with difficulty lies a field of fantasy. sf maintains a respect for fact or presumptive fact, fantasy makes a point of flouting these.

Fantasy story could be turned into sf story. Although vampirism is one of the staples of 19th century fantasy, Richard Matheson's novel "I am legend" makes brilliantly ingenious and horrifying use of the myth for sf purpose and whereby every traditional detail is explained along rational lines.

The extract continues on this page, followed by Kingsley Amis's short note on science fiction and fantasy

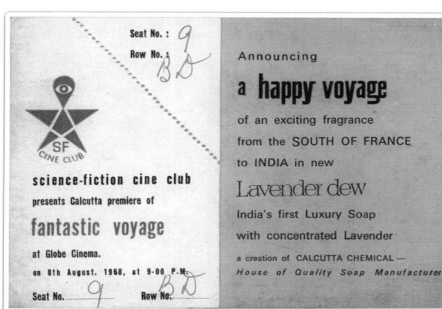

Invitation cards for Sci-Fi Cine Club film-show of *Fantastic Voyage*, designed by Ray in 1968

Above: Envelope of the invitation card designed by Satyajit Ray. *Below:* The envelope which contained the film brochure

20TH CENTURY-FOX Presents

fantastic voyage

"It really needs a superb imagination to create such a movie and watching it was a delight. The structure of the various organs shown was true to the smallest detail. I am sure this picture would be enjoyed not only by the medical profession and medical students but by students of biology at all levels."
Dr. B. C. Mehta
M.D., M.R.C.P.

"To me viewing "FANTASTIC VOYAGE" has been an unforgettable experience. What impressed me most was the scientific accuracy with which such a fantastically improbable theme was presented as plausible possibility in the not too far distant future."
V. V. Da Silva
M.S. (Bom.) F.R.C.S. (Eng.)
Prof. of Surgery,
Grant Medical College

make a last desperate dash for the thrombus lodged "less than half a degree off-center in the midbrain."

Do the scientists complete their mission? How do they get out of Benes' body? — Answers to these questions are found in the films's stunning climactic scenes.

This then is the unique theme of "Fantastic Voyage" — an adventure of astonishing suspense and beauty. It takes you where no film camera has ever been before. Fantastic? — Yes! But, in this world of ours, where heart-transplants are done, where travelling to the moon will soon be a reality, some day, perhaps tomorrow the Fantastic events that you will see, can and will take place.

We are extremely happy that many leading men of medicine have seen and acclaimed "Fantastic Voyage" and found its viewing beneficial to both practitioners and students.

We urge you to see "Fantastic Voyage"

fantastic voyage

STARRING
Stephen Boyd, Raquel Welch, Edmond O'Brien, Donald Pleasence, Arthur O'Connell, William Redfield and Arthur Kennedy. Produced by Saul David. Directed by Richard Fleischer. Screenplay by Harry Kleiner, Adaptation by David Duncan. Music by Leonard Rosenman, Cinemascope, Color by DeLuxe. 20.

GLOBE

FROM FRIDAY AUG. 9, '68
Daily at 3, 6, 9 P. M. (U)

The folder of *Fantastic Voyage* specifically made for its release

LETTER FROM BRADBURY

Bradbury   10265 Cheviot Drive   Los Angeles 64.
California, USA.

February 12th, 1963

Dear Mr. Ray:

Your good letter has at last been passed on to me
from Playboy, in Chicago, and I want to thank you
for your appreciation of my work. Yes, I know
your name very well, and have heard wondrous things
about your trilogy, your Apu films, in the last
few years.

I will make this reply of mine very short, for
I wish to go over my stories in great detail and
think about them, and then write you again in
about one week, when I have had time to select
a few stories to send to you, along with my
reasons for thinking you might also enjoy them.

It is true that Truffaut is proceeding with
Fahrenheit 451, which is tremendously exciting for
me. Simultaneously, Jean-Louis Barrault is
scheduling a play based on my MARTIAN CHRONICLES
for October, in Paris.

It is heartening to hear of your interest in
science-fiction. I agree, it is long past time
for much to be done in motion pictures in this
field.

You'll hear from me again, quickly. Meantime,
would it be possible for you, through your
release organization in Hollywood, to arrange for
me to see your Trilogy? I would welcome the
opportunity to see them in sequence during a
single week. If this is troublesome, please wait
to move on it.

Again, your letter has made me very happy.
I send you my best wishes,

Sincerely,

Ray Bradbury

Telephone: 94255, 598730
Cable: UNDERSEA
COLOMBO

දුරකථනය: 94255, 598730

ARTHUR C. CLARKE

"LESLIE'S HOUSE"
25, BARNES PLACE, COLOMBO 7, SRI LANKA

ආතර් සි ක්ලාක්
"ලෙස්ලිගෙ නිවස"
25, බාන්ස්පෙදෙස, කොළඹ 7, ශ්‍රී ලංකාව

Mr. Satyajit Ray,   2nd. Oct. 1987
1/1 Bishop Lefroy Rd.,
Calcutta 20,
India.

Dear Satyajit,

    Many thanks for sending "The Unicorn Expedition" which I
enjoyed reading. I hope you don't mind my inability to write the
introduction but I am completely overwhelmed and now have a
serious medical problem. (see enclosed form) Incidentally I am
very happy to hear that you are back in harness but hope you
don't over do it.

    I enjoyed the stories very much particularly the Night of
the Indigo.†

    You'll be amused to know that Mike A.K.A. Swami Sivakalki
dropped in this morning - I've not seen him for quite a while -he
sends his regards!

    My best wishes for all your activities.

        As ever,

            atc.

*It made me cry - my Rex is
buried in the garden.*

The accompanying photograph
was enclosed with the letter

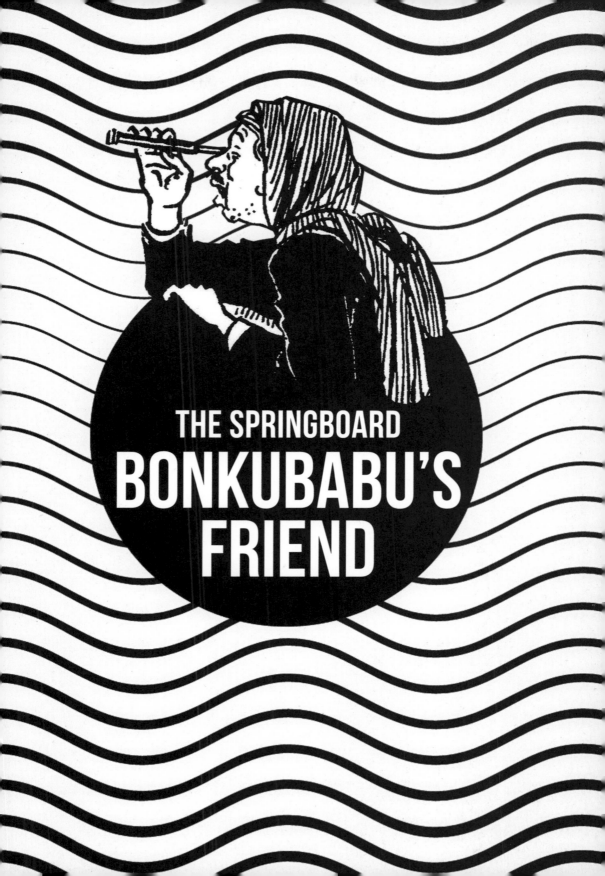

THE SPRINGBOARD
BONKUBABU'S FRIEND

BONKUBABU'S FRIEND

Satyajit Ray

Sandesh, February 1962

No one had ever seen Bonkubabu getting annoyed. In fact, it would be very difficult to predict what exactly he would do if he ever got really angry.

It is not as if there were never any reasons for him to get cross. For the past twenty-two years he had been teaching geography and Bengali at the Kankurgachhi Primary School. Over the years numerous batches of pupils had appeared in his class, and playing pranks on Bonkubabu—drawing his portrait on the blackboard, adding glue on his chair, or even setting off firecrackers next to him on the night of Kali puja—had become a part of the school's longstanding tradition.

None of this provoked Bonkubabu. On a few occasions he would only clear his throat and say, "Shame on you, children!" But he never ever lost his cool.

One reason for taking such a stand was that he felt if he ever gave in to a fit of rage, it wouldn't be easy for him, at his advanced age, to find another job. The other reason he never gave in to anger was that even among a class full of wayward students there were always a few good, intelligent students and Bonkubabu found immense pleasure in teaching them. For him, his vocation was not just fulfilling, but rewarding as well. At times, he would invite some of these students home after school. Then, having offered them refreshments, he would read out stories of faraway lands and thrilling adventures. He would talk of life in Africa; of the discovery of the North Pole; about human-flesh-eating fish in Brazil; and about Atlantis, the continent submerged under the sea. As Bonkubabu was an excellent raconteur, his students listened to these stories with rapt attention.

On weekend evenings, Bonkubabu would make his way to the house of the village councillor, Sripati Majumdar. Here, friends and neighbours generally got together for tea and conversation. Very often he toyed with the idea of never returning the next weekend.

Headpiece illustration by Satyajit Ray for "Bonkubabur Bandhu" in *Sandesh*

While he could somehow put up with the pranks played by his students, he could not suffer the ridicule these grown-ups heaped on him. The kind of jokes and taunts he was subjected to at these gatherings often tested the limit of his endurance.

Just the other day, for example, a couple of months ago, they were talking about ghosts. Bonkubabu usually did not say much during these discussions. But that day something seemed to have happened to him—he blurted out that ghosts had never frightened him. Lo and behold! Who would let go of such an opportunity? While returning home later that night, Bonkubabu suffered heavily. One thin, spooky figure smeared in black ink leaped at him from the tamarind tree. Clearly, this was a very carefully planned attack.

The "haunting" didn't scare him. But it left him injured. His neck ached for three days. And what's worse—his new kurta didn't just tear; it was stained black. You call this a joke?

If this was not enough, other mischiefs were played on him at regular intervals— hiding his shoes and umbrellas; replacing the stuffing of his paan with soil; bullying him to sing…

Despite these travails, he had to mark his presence at the get-together. Or else what would Sripatibabu think? Not only was he a respected figure in the village, he also seemed to desire Bonkubabu's presence. In Sripatibabu's mind, what was the point of a gathering if you couldn't tease someone for some entertainment? Bonkubabu unwittingly filled that need and was thus invariably summoned.

The subject for today's gathering was rather of a high level. Or in other words, satellites were being discussed. This evening, a little after sunset, a moving light had been spotted in the northern sky. Three months ago, a similar light had been spotted, which became a subject of much speculation. Later, it was discovered that it was a Russian satellite. This was named "khotka" (doubt) or could be a "phoshka" (blister)! Apparently, this satellite had been orbiting Earth at a height of 400 miles. It offered scientists a wealth of information.

This evening it was Bonkubabu who first spotted this odd light. Having done so he brought it to the notice of Nidhu Moktar. But when he arrived at the meeting, Bonkubabu realized that Nidhu Moktar had taken full credit for being the first one to spot it and was thoroughly enjoying the limelight. Bonkubabu decided to stay quiet.

No one seems to know much about satellites in this part of the world. But what is there to stop them from discussing it? Chandibabu said, "Whatever the case, I feel it's quite pointless to pay so much attention to this. To me it's the same as spotting the gemstone on a snake's head. In some obscure corner of the sky you catch a glimpse of a strange light, the press goes gaga reporting this. While reading this report you gloat over it, sitting in your sofa, chewing a paan. As if all this adds to your credit, your pride. You deserve the applause. Huh!"

Ramkanai, a younger voice, contradicted him. "No, it may not be one of us, but the credit goes to human achievement after all, doesn't it? And that's some achievement!"

Chandibabu retorted, "Well … well … of course it's a human endeavour. Do you expect a bunch of monkeys to achieve this? Would you?"

Nidhu Moktar now offered his view. "That's fine. Leave the satellite alone. After all it's only a machine, devoid of any human presence which is mechanically going round and round the Earth. So does any spinning toy. The ceiling fan too starts rotating the moment you switch it on. No big deal. But what about a rocket? You can't be indifferent to a rocket, dear chaps."

Twitching his nostrils, Chandibabu remarked, "So, what's so great about a rocket? It would still make some sense if it's made in our own country and takes off from our local field for the moon. Then we all can go buy tickets to watch the spectacle … well, that'll make some point."

"You're right," Ramkanai said. "In reality, rockets make no sense to us."

Bhairav Chakravarty chimed in, "Suppose something arrives from another planet…"

"Even so, we both won't be able to see this after all."

"Yes, that's true enough."

Then they all focused on their teacups. Enough had already been said.

Amidst this silence Bonkubabu cleared his throat and muttered, "Suppose it arrives here?"

Trying to look surprised, Nidhubabu said, "Just listen to what this flapdoodle has to say! Who'll come here? And from where, I pray?"

In a near whisper, Bonkubabu said, "Suppose some being from a different planet comes here…"

As was his habit, Bhairav Chakravarty landed a bold slap on Bonkubabu's back, and with a toothy grin exclaimed, "Bravo! Bonkubihari, bravo! People from other planets will land up here? In this remote corner? Not London, not Moscow, not New York, not even Calcutta. Straight away here in Kankurgachhi? In this godforsaken place? That's some wishful thinking, I say!"

Bonkubabu remained silent. But he pondered over this. Well, it was not absolutely unfeasible! If one was arriving from the outer world, the ultimate mission would be to arrive on Earth. How did it matter where they arrived? Just as it was improbable for them to land in Kankurgachhi, it was equally possible for them to land here. Who knows!

Till now Sripatibabu hadn't opened his mouth. But when he shifted his position in his chair everyone turned to him. He put down his teacup on the table and with conviction opined, "If at all someone from a different planet comes, I can tell you that they certainly won't land up in this wretched place. Don't they have anything better to do? And they are certainly no fools. I've a strong feeling that they are of Caucasian origin and will definitely land up in a Western country. Right?"

With the sole exception of Bonkubabu everyone agreed.

Taking the point further, silently pointing at Bonkubabu, Chandibabu poked Nidhu Moktar and said in all innocence, "Well, Bonkubabu can jolly well be right, you know. It would be quite normal for them to turn up here in the presence of our flapdoodle? What do you say, Nidhubabu? Suppose they need to collect a specimen from here, what can be a better one than him?"

Approving wholeheartedly, Nidhu Moktar chipped in, "Oh yes, oh yes. Be it his looks, brains, mind, this sample would be the ideal one!"

"A perfect example to be preserved in a museum or zoo," added Ramkanai.

Bonkubabu thought to himself—if one talks of specimens, aren't they equally suitable? Look at that Sripatibabu—the chin so resembles a camel's. And that Bhairav Chakravarty—his eyes are so much like that of a tortoise; Nidhu Moktar so wonderfully resembles a mole; Ramkanai is rather like a goat; Chandibabu is just like a flitter mouse. How well they all deserve a place in the zoo!

Bonkubabu's eyes welled up. He got up to leave. He had hoped so much to enjoy himself this evening. But alas, that was not to be.

"Already leaving? So soon?" Sripatibabu enquired, as if much concerned.

"Yes, it's getting rather late."

"Late? Is it that late? Hah! In any case tomorrow's a holiday. Just sit back, relax and enjoy another cup of tea."

"Many thanks, but I must go. I have to mark papers tonight. Namaskar."

Ramkanai warned, "Be careful, Bonkuda. Today happens to be a new moon night. And it's a Saturday. Very inviting for ghosts and goblins."

***

Bonkubabu noticed the beam only when he was midway into Poncha Ghosh's bamboo grove. He wasn't carrying any light. And as it was winter he had no fear that he would encounter snakes. Also, he was used to this route. Though most people did not take this road, Bonkubabu had often used it as a shortcut. In the last few minutes something had been bothering him. But he couldn't pinpoint the exact source of his unease. Suddenly he realized there was no noise coming from the crickets. They had fallen completely silent. And that made all the difference. Usually the deeper he walked into the grove the chirpier they became. Today it was just the opposite. And hence this eerie atmosphere. Buy why? Had all the crickets gone to sleep?

Perplexed, he continued to walk and after twenty yards or so he noticed the light. At first, he thought perhaps there was a fire in the bamboo grove. Right in the middle of the grove, in the clearing near the small pond, a pink glow reflected on the nearby leaves, twigs and branches. And down below that, right on the pond the light glimmered. But it was no fire: It was a constant, still light.

Bonkubabu continued to walk.

In a while his ears began ringing. It was a sound which one cannot describe, somewhat like the sound you hear when your ears feel blocked. A loud buzzing noise. Though Bonkubabu shivered in fright, he continued to move on along the growth of the bamboo stems, thanks to his indomitable curiosity.

And suddenly he came upon a sight that opened his eyes wide in shock: an upturned bowl almost covered the entire pond. A pink glow was emitting from this translucent giant body which reflected on the outside area as well.

Not even in his wildest dreams had Bonkubabu imagined such an extraordinary object.

After spending a few seconds in a daze, he noticed that though the object remained still, it seemed as if it wasn't quite lifeless. There was a constant glimmer emitting from it. It looked as though the glass mound was slowly rising and falling, just as a human chest heaves when breathing.

This illustration appeared in 1970 for the book *Ek Dojon Goppo* (One Dozen Stories) in which "Bonkubabur Bandhu" was included

To take a closer look, Bonkubabu stepped forward and suddenly he felt as though an electric current had passed through his body. Some unknown power had rendered him completely immobile. He was left with no strength. He could move neither forward nor backward.

After standing in this stiff position for a while Bonkubabu noticed that the object had gradually stopped "breathing" and the ear-splitting humming noise had stopped too. A second later, shattering the silence of the night, a very thin, piercing voice, almost human in sound, uttered: *milipipping khruk ... milipipping khruk...!*

This startled Bonkubabu. What sort of a language was this? And where was this voice coming from? Where was the speaker concealed?

Bonkubabu's heart jumped when the same voice spoke again.

"Who are you? Who are you?"

Oh dear, this was in English! Were the words being spoken to him?

Bonkubabu gulped and replied, "I'm Bonkubihari Dutta, sir, Bonkubihari Dutta."

"Are you English? Are you English?" the voice continued.

"No, sir!" he shouted back. "Bengali, sir, a Bengali Kayastha."

There was a distinct pause. Then the voice clearly said, "Namaskar!"

Heaving a sigh of relief, Bonkubabu greeted back, "Namaskar." In that instant he felt that the invisible tie that had fastened him so tightly had become loose. He could have easily run away but did not. Because just then, much to his astonishment, he noticed that a section of this large mound was sliding open from one side like a door.

From that door emerged a head like that of a smooth ball. Followed by the figure of the weirdest creature he had ever seen in his life.

Except for the head, its entire body was wrapped in a shiny pink material. The face showed two holes in place of ears and another hole made up the nose and the mouth. The body was devoid of any hair or fur. Its deep-set eyes were yellow, glowing in the dark.

The being slowly approached Bonkubabu, stopped a few feet away and gave him a steady look with his unblinking pair of eyes. Bonkubabu found himself folding his hands in a namaskar.

After observing him for almost a minute, once more in that high-pitched voice sounding more like a flute, the being said, "Are you human?"

"Yes."

"Is this Earth?"

"Yes."

"I see. So, my guess was quite right. My gadgets are not working properly. I meant to visit Pluto. As I wasn't sure where I landed, I first questioned you in the language spoken in Pluto. When I received no reply from you I realized I must have landed on Earth. What a waste of time and energy! This has happened to me once before. Instead of going to Mars I got diverted to Jupiter. All my plans got delayed by one whole day, you see! Ha ha ha."

Bonkubabu didn't know how to react. As it is he was feeling very uncomfortable. Because the being was examining his arms and legs with his long, bony fingers.

After finishing this exercise, the being introduced itself: "I'm Ang from the planet Craneus. I am infinitely superior to man."

Must I believe him! This four-foot scrawny figure is superior to a man? Bonkubabu laughed to himself.

Ang read his mind instantly. He said, "Don't be so sceptical. I can prove it. How many languages do you know?"

Bonkubabu scratched his head and replied, "Bengali, English … umm … a bit of Hindi."

"You mean two and a half?"

"I suppose so."

"I know fourteen thousand. There isn't a single language spoken in this solar system that I don't know about. In addition to this, I know thirty-one languages spoken on planets outside this system. I've personally been to all these twenty-five planets. How old are you?"

"I'm fifty."

"I'm eight hundred and thirty-three. Do you eat animals?"

Bonkubabu had recently relished meat curry during the Kali puja celebrations. How could he deny this?

"We've stopped eating meat for the last few hundred years," Ang disclosed. "Before that we used to consume the meat of many creatures. I might then have eaten you."

Bonkubabu swallowed nervously.

"Have you seen this?"

Ang placed a pebble-like small stone in Bonkubabu's hand. The moment Bonkubabu touched it, an electric current passed through his body once more. Frightened, he immediately returned the pebble to Ang.

Ang smiled and said, "Because of this object in my hand you couldn't move at all. No one can. This would stop anyone from getting closer. Nothing can be more effective in rendering an enemy immobile without actually harming him."

This time Bonkubabu was really taken by surprise.

Ang said, "Is there any place you wish to visit or a scene you'd aspire to see but you could never do so?"

Bonkubabu thought—well, I wish to see the entire world! He was a teacher of geography yet he hadn't seen anything beyond a couple of villages and cities of Bengal. In fact, what else had he seen within Bengal itself? He was yet to see the snow-capped mountains of the Himalayas, the sea in Digha, the forest of Sunderbans … In fact even that well-known banyan tree in nearby Shibpur.

Not revealing any of these thoughts to Ang, he only said, "I want to see and visit so many things but coming from a warm climate, most of all what I desire is to visit the North Pole."

Ang took out a tube with a glass attached to its one end, not unlike a telescope, and placed it in front of Bonkubabu. "Just look through this," invited Ang. As Bonkubabu peered through one end he got goosebumps. Was this for real? An endless expanse of snow stretched out before him. Up above, the deep blue sky formed changing patterns in streamers of light in the colours of the rainbow. The Aurora Borealis! Now, what was that—an igloo! And there was a row of polar bears. The appearance of yet another animal. What was this peculiar animal? After a closer look he realized it was a walrus. Not just

Illustration by Ray, *Sandesh*, 1962

one, there were two of them and they were engaged in a fierce fight! They were attacking each other with their tusks. It reminded him so much of radishes—streams of blood flowed over the soft white snow...

Despite the cold of December, Bonkubabu broke into a sweat.

"Don't you wish to go to Brazil?" asked Ang.

One instant association struck Bonkubabu—those dreaded carnivorous piranha fish. That's strange! How on earth could Ang guess what he would like to see?

Once more Bonkubabu looked through the tube. This time he saw a dense forest. The sun was trying to break through this impenetrable wood hesitantly. He spotted an enormous tree and hanging from its branch—now what's that? Oh Christ! He could not even imagine a snake of this proportion. Suddenly a thought flashed through his mind—Brazil's anaconda! He'd once read about it somewhere. In size it was considered to be much superior to a python. But what about the fish? Ah, a canal with crocodiles sleeping in the sun on both sides of the bank. One of them moved. It was planning to go into the water. It dashed! Bonkubabu could even hear the sound of a splash. But what happened? Why had the crocodile jumped out of the water at such an alarming speed? But was it the same crocodile? Bonkubabu's eyes popped out—he noticed that nothing was left of the reptile's abdomen. All the flesh was gone and the bones were clearly showing through it. And still attached to the rest of the body were five fish with sharp teeth feeding on with ravenous appetite. Piranhas!

Bonkubabu could not take it any more. His limbs were trembling ... his head was reeling...

"Are you now convinced that we're superior?" proclaimed Ang.

Bonkubabu ran his tongue over his dry lips. "Oh, yes, of course. Certainly. Definitely!" He groaned.

"Ah well," remarked Ang. "I've been observing you. After feeling your arms and limbs, I realize you're of a much inferior breed. However, for a mere human you're not so bad. But your main limitation is you're far too meek and mild. No wonder you haven't achieved much in life. Why just you, every living being ought to speak up against injustice and insinuations aimed at them, especially if it's unprovoked. Though there was no plan to meet you in my scheme of things, I have enjoyed meeting you. However, frankly, I don't wish to waste any more time on Earth. I shall leave now."

"Goodbye, Mr Ang," said Bonkubabu and continued, "I, too, was so fortunate to have..."

Bonkubabu couldn't complete his sentence. In a nanosecond, before he could grasp the scenario, Ang had stepped back into the spaceship and had already flown over Poncha Ghosh's bamboo grove and vanished. As silence descended once more within the grove, Bonkubabu realized that the crickets were back to chirping. It was getting rather late.

Bonkubabu resumed his walk back home. His mind was in turmoil. Slowly he began to comprehend the full impact of this event. One anonymous man—no, not quite—an Ang had appeared from some unknown planet and met him. How extraordinary! How unbelievable! Amidst countless people in this world he had been the chosen one. Bonkubihari Dutta, a teacher of geography and Bengali in Kankurgachhi Primary School. From now on, at least in this regard, he would remain matchless in this universe.

Bonkubabu felt that he was no longer walking. He was flying!

The next day was a Sunday. As always, the meeting at Sripatibabu's house was on in full swing. Newspapers had reported this incident but only as a minor occurrence. A strange light had been seen by a handful of people in only two areas of Bengal. This occurrence was typically associated with the sighting of flying saucers.

Tonight, Poncha Ghosh too was present. He was describing the present status of his bamboo grove. About ten bamboo trees around the pond had shed their leaves overnight. It was natural for them to shed their leaves in winter, but for only a few of them to go bare all at once was rather an unusual happening. While this was being discussed, Bhairav Chakravarty suddenly inquired, "Why is Bonku so late today?"

That's true! How come no one had noticed his absence so far?

Nidhu Moktar said, "I don't think Bonku will turn up today after that earful he received from us yesterday."

With alacrity Sripatibabu commented, "No, you can't get away saying this. We need Bonku. Ramkanai, why don't you go and fetch him?"

Ramkanai said he would do so only after he finished his tea. He was about to take another sip when Bonkubabu entered the room.

No, it would be wrong to say a man "entered". What entered was a tornado, sweeping in, in the form of a short dark man, startling everyone present in the room. His entry turned the setting topsy-turvy. He burst into an uproarious laughter and continued to laugh for one whole minute—something no one had heard or seen before. Not even Bonkubabu himself.

When he could finally stop, he cleared his throat and began to speak in a commanding voice: "Friends! With utmost happiness I hereby announce that this is going to be my final day at these meetings. I'm here today chiefly because I want to tell you all a few things before I leave for good. Number one—this holds true for everyone— you all speak such utter rubbish. Only idiots debate on matters they know nothing about. Number two—this is for Chandibabu—at your age the idea of hiding other people's shoes and umbrellas is absolutely disgusting, apart from being childish. Kindly return my umbrella and my brown canvas shoes to me and deposit them at my house. Nidhubabu— if you continue to call me flapdoodle, I'll in return call you a nincompoop. Please accept this gracefully. And Sripatibabu—you're a noted figure of this village and you ought to be surrounded by toadies. But from today I choose not to be part of this group. In fact, I can send my tomcat who's extremely good at licking feet. Ah yes—I can also spot Ponchababu here—let me give you as well as others this news—from the planet Craneus a being called Ang landed on the pond in your bamboo grove last night. We met and had a long chat. That fellow … oops … the Ang … was most affable."

After delivering his monologue, Bonkubabu clapped his hand so hard on Bhairav Chakravarty's back that the gentleman began to choke. With strident steps, Bonkubabu then made a grand exit; leaving everyone goggle-eyed with disbelief.

And at that instant the cup slipped from Ramkanai's hand, smashing into pieces and splashing hot tea on everyone's clothes.

Translated from the Bengali by **INDRANI MAJUMDAR**

BONKUBABU'S FRIEND: TV SERIES SCRIPT

Script by Satyajit Ray, directed by Sandip Ray

Satyajit Ray Presents 2, Doordarshan, 1986

Principal Characters
BONKUBABU, a school teacher
MR CHOWDHURY, a rich man
ANG, the alien

PART I

Day. Interior of a classroom (Class X).
BONKUBIHARI DUTTA, *the geography teacher, is taking his class.*
BONKU: The jungles in the Amazon are among the densest in the world.
They are full of strange plants and animals. For instance, there
is a fish there that has sharp teeth and lives on animal flesh. Does
anyone know what this fish is called?
(*One of the boys,* SUMAN, *raises his hand.*) BONKU: Yes, Suman?
SUMAN: Piranha, sir. The fish is called piranha.
BONKU: Very good. How did you know about it?
SUMAN: I read about it in a book on South America.
BONKU: That's very good. Now, you have seen pictures of penguins. Do you
know where you can find these birds?

(*Another hand is raised. It is* RANEN.)

BONKU: Yes, Ranen?

RANEN: In the South Pole.

BONKU: That's right. In the Antarctic. The fact that we live in a remote corner of Bihar does not mean that we should not know about the wonders of the planet that we inhabit. There are books and there are pictures. Geography is not a collection of dry facts. It has to do with living things too. The Himalayas are supposed to be young mountains which are still growing. I haven't seen the Himalayas myself, but I feel a great thrill when I read about it. Not just because it belongs to Asia. I feel the same thrill about the polar regions, about the forests and mountains of Africa where the gorillas live, and about the caravans of camels in the Sahara.

RAJIV (a pupil): But, sir, how much better it would be if we could see these things with our own eyes!

BONKU: No doubt about it. Who knows, one of you may grow up to be an explorer—although I must be content with my lot as a schoolmaster, and derive as much pleasure as is possible from my books and my imagination.

(*The bell rings.* BONKU *gets up, and so do the boys.*)

BONKU: In my next class, I shall tell you about life in the depths of the ocean. I have been reading a book about it. It is fascinating.

VILLAGE STREET. EVENING.

BONKU *walks homeward, carrying a load of examination papers. He stops to light a* bidi. *His attention is caught by something in the sky. He stops.*

From his point of view, a moving light is seen in the sky. It is about the size of Venus.

BONKU *follows it, fascinated.*

NIDHIRAM *the pleader, who is walking by, stops to ask:*

What are you looking at the sky for?

BONKU: Just look at that moving light.

(NIDHIRAM *looks up.*)

NIDHIRAM: Oh yes, I can see that. I wonder what it is.

BONKU: Must be a satellite or something.

NIDHI: Must be.

(NIDHIRAM *has lost interest in the light.*)

NIDHI: You're coming to Mr Chowdhury's, I hope.

BONKU: I haven't made up my mind yet. Look at all these examination papers.

NIDHI: Don't be absurd. You know Mr Chowdhury expects you.

BONKU: Yes, I know. He needs someone who will put up with his sarcasm without a murmur. I know I am the butt of his jokes.

NIDHI: Well, you must consider yourself lucky. After all, Mr Chowdhury is the wealthiest and most powerful man in the village. You must come.

BONKU: I suppose I will.

NIDHI: Well, see you later then.

BONKU: See you later.

(NIDHIRAM *goes away.* BONKU *takes another look at the moving light and continues homeward.*)

BONKUBABU'S RESIDENCE.

BONKUBABU *knocks on the door, which is opened by his servant* DAYAL.

BONKU *enters.*

BONKU: My cup of tea, Dayal.

DAYAL: Very well, sir.

BONKUBABU'S SITTING ROOM AND STUDY.

BONKU *puts down the books on the table, wipes his perspiration with his dhoti. His eye is caught by a framed picture on the wall—Mt. Everest.* BONKU *now walks to the window and looks out at the evening sky. He sees the moving light again. This time it looks slightly bigger and brighter.*

MR CHOWDHURY'S DRAWING ROOM.

CHOWDHURY, *who looks the rich, zamindar type, reclines on a divan with his elbow on a bolster, smoking a gargara. There are five other men in the room, seated on the ground on which a white cloth is spread. They are, of course, on a lower level from* CHOWDHURY.

CHOWDHURY: Satellite?

NIDHI: That's what it seemed like.

CHOWDHURY: Was the light moving very fast?

NIDHI: No. In fact, rather slowly.

CHOWDHURY: So it can't be a meteor.

NIDHI: Oh, no, sir. It moved much slower than a meteor.

CHOWDHURY: Has anyone else seen it?

NIDHI: I was the first to see it, and I pointed it out to Bonkubihari.

CHOWDHURY: What does he have to say? Where is Bonku? Why is he so late today?

(*At this point* BONKUBABU *enters and sits diffidently in a corner of the room.*)

CHOWDHURY: Ah, there you are! You will live a hundred years. We had just mentioned your name.

BONKU: Is that so?

CHOWDHURY: Nidhiram had just mentioned about the light in the sky he had pointed out to you.

BONKU: Which *he* had pointed out to *me*?

NIDHI: Don't you remember—I called out to you?

BONKU: Oh yes, I see. Yes, of course.

CHOWDHURY: Well, we are anxious to know what you feel about it.

BONKU: Well, it may be one of the Soviet or American satellites. There are so many of them circling Earth now.

RAMKANAI: It could be a spaceship from another planet. I was reading a story the other day about such a spaceship.

BHAIRAB: May I ask you what it is doing in the skies above Lochanpur in this godforsaken corner of the earth? I suppose you believe that it wants to land here?

(RAMKANAI *is flustered.*)

RAMKANAI: Oh, I was just thinking aloud. I didn't really mean it.

BONKU: But I think it's a very good idea. I have also read in the papers about spaceships from other planets—shaped like a saucer. Flying saucers, they're called.

BHAIRAB: But what would a flying saucer be doing in Lochanpur? I suppose you think they have come to land here?

BONKU: What is so unusual about that?

NIDHI: A spaceship from another planet landing in Lochanpur? You think there's nothing unusual about that?

BONKU: Well, they have come to land on Earth. They don't know about London, New York, Moscow, Paris, Tokyo and all the big cities. Why shouldn't they land in Lochanpur? This is just as good as any other place.

RAMKANAI: I know. I think they've come to visit Bonkubabu.

BHAIRAB: Exactly, they have come to collect human specimens, and what better specimen than Bonku? What do you say, Nidhi?

NIDHI: Perfect. Why, just look at him. Eyes full of intelligence and wisdom. Forehead like Shakespeare's. Nose like a Greek god's. It's all perfect.

A BAMBOO GROVE.
A spaceship emanating a pink glow descends in a clearing.
BONKU's *room.*
The wall with the picture of Everest is lit up momentarily with the pink glow.

MR CHOWDHURY'S DRAWING ROOM.
The servant brings tea, which is handed round to everybody. CHOWDHURY *speaks at last.*

CHOWDHURY: I think we are wasting our time talking about spaceships. People from other planets are sahibs, and if they were to land on Earth, they would land on European soil. I am convinced about that. Now, Bonku, what about that song you promised us the other evening? Ramkanai, push that harmonium towards him. (RAMKANAI *does as told, but* BONKU *is aghast.*)

BONKU: But I never made a promise like that, sir. How could I, when I know nothing about singing?

BHAIRAB: But I heard you humming a bhajan the other day.

BONKU: But everybody hums—that doesn't mean that I can sing.

CHOWDHURY: There's no use trying to be modest. You must give us a song today.

EVERYBODY: Yes, you must, you must.

(BONKU *seems to yield to pressure.*)

BONKU: But I don't know how to play the harmonium.

CHOWDHURY: Well, sing without it, then.

(*A silence falls in the room. A minute later,* BONKU *begins to sing a bhajan—if it can be called singing.*)

BONKU: "Mainey chakar rakho ji...'

(*"Wan, wah" from everybody. But* BONKU *can sing only two lines, and then has to stop—humiliation forcing tears from his eyes. There is silence in the room.*)

CHOWDHURY: What kind of a person are you? You have spoilt the mood of the evening!

(BONKU *suddenly gets up and leaves the room. The others sit still.*)

PART II

EVENING.

BONKU *makes his way home through a path in the bamboo grove. Everything is very quiet, except for the chirping of crickets.* BONKU *enters deeper into the forest. There is a faint trace of light still in the evening sky.*

Suddenly the chirping of crickets grows dim in volume and gradually disappears. Now there is an unearthly stillness.

Suddenly BONKU *spots through the bamboos an area which is lighted. What is happening there?*

Prompted by curiosity, BONKU *advances towards the lighted area. As he crosses a screen of bamboos, he sees something lying half-submerged in a pit in an opening in the bamboo grove. It is shaped like an inverted saucer and is made of some translucent material. Through this material a pink glow emerges and lights up the area around.* BONKU *has stopped, but curiosity gets the better of him and he advances.*

The pink light is pulsating, but as BONKU *arrives within five yards of the object, the pulsation ceases and the light becomes steady.*

BONKU *stops puzzled. Then he steps back and the rhythmic pulsation begins again. But as* BONKU *advances again and reaches the point he had reached before, the light becomes steady.*

BONKU *now stays put and awaits developments.*

There are five beeps. Then silence. Then a high-pitched metallic voice is heard.

VOICE: Good evening.

(BONKU *says nothing. He is so excited he almost trembles. The voice now continues.*)

VOICE: *Bonjour! ... Buona sera! ... Guten abend! ...* (in Chinese) … (in Russian) ... Namaste!

BONKU: (*hastily*) Namaste!

(*There is a pause. Now the voice resumes, speaking in Hindi.*)

VOICE: This is Earth?

BONKU: Yes, sir.

VOICE: You are an Indian?

BONKU: Yes, sir.

VOICE: Do you have a name?

BONKU: Yes, sir.

VOICE: What is it?

BONKU: Bonkubihari Dutta, sir.

VOICE: Bonkubihari Dutta?

BONKU: Yes, sir.

VOICE: What is your profession?

BONKU: I am a schoolmaster.

VOICE: Schoolmaster?

BONKU: Yes, sir.

VOICE: You teach?

BONKU: Yes, sir.

VOICE: What do you teach?

BONKU: Geography, sir.

VOICE: Geography of the Earth?

BONKU: Yes, sir. We don't know enough about other planets.

VOICE: Have you heard of Craenius?

BONKU: No, sir.

VOICE: I am Ang, from the planet Craenius. We belong to a different solar system.

BONKU: I see.

ANG: Your civilization goes back five thousand years?

BONKU: Yes, sir.

ANG: Ours goes back a million years.

BONKU: I see, sir.

ANG: Do you mind if I come out and take a look at you?

BONKU: Oh no, sir. And I would like to see you very much.

(*Now there is a hum from a machinery, and the top of the spaceship opens out like the petals of a flower. Through the opening emerges a creature with a large head and spindly limbs. The body is encased in a space suit though the head is bare. The eyes are a couple of glowing white balls.*

Now the creature jumps from the top of the spaceship and lands in slow motion on the grass ten feet away from BONKU,

ANG *slowly approaches* BONKU, *who stands stiffly in one spot.* ANG *stops three feet away from* BONKU *and closely observes him. At last he speaks…*)

ANG: H'm—two eyes, two ears, two nostrils, two lips, two arms, two legs—just as I had anticipated.

(ANG *now prods* BONKU's *body with his three fingers. He places his hand over* BONKU's *heart and immediately the heartbeats are heard loudly.* ANG *removes his hand and the sound stops.*)

Make-up artist Ananta Das prepares Ang played by Satu Mukherjee in the TV Series. Photographs courtesy Nemai Ghosh

ANG: H'm—average. Average intelligence, average constitution, average appetite, average looks…

(BONKU *says nothing.*)

ANG: And yet you are an ambitious man! You aspire to see the great mountains, the great oceans, the great forests and the deserts of the earth.

BONKU: Yes, yes, sir! I only read about them in the books and look at the pictures. It fires my imagination, but I can do nothing about it.

ANG: Do you want to see what these places actually look like?

BONKU: Oh yes, sir!

(ANG *now produces from the air a tube and hands it to* BONKU.)

ANG: Look through that and tell me what you can see.

(BONKU *does as told and gasps in amazement.*)

BONKU: I see snow. Why, it is the Antarctic, because I see penguins. (*We also see what* BONKU *sees.*)

ANG: And now what do you see?

BONKU: Trees—a dense forest … looks like a tropical rain forest.

ANG: Those are the Amazonian jungles.

BONKU: But the view is changing.

ANG: I know. I am making it change. What do you see now?

BONKU: A camel caravan in a desert. Why, there are the pyramids in the background! It is the Sahara! How wonderful!

ANG: Well, you may keep this tube. But remember—it will work only with you and no one else.

BONKU: Thank you, Mr Ang, thank you!

ANG: But tell me one thing.

BONKU: Yes—

ANG: Why are you so submissive? Why do you always yield to pressure? And why do you always put up with people making fun of you?

BONKU: Sir, I am a poor man. I have to keep my job—or my family will starve.

ANG: It is a crime to swallow insult. It is a crime where I come from.

BONKU: Sir, if you could advise me what I should do.

ANG: Are you a good teacher?

BONKU: I think so, sir.

ANG: You are useful and necessary to your school.

BONKU: I believe I am.

ANG: Then no one can take away your job. You must assert yourself. I won't tell you how. As soon as you have the courage you will know what to do. Remember you are no longer just a poor schoolmaster. You have just had an experience which no one in this planet has had. That makes you unique, doesn't it? This alone should give you courage.

BONKU: Yes, yes, I think so.

ANG: Very well then, I must say goodbye now. My machine is repaired, and I must be on my way to my destination. I am very pleased to have made your acquaintance, Bonkubihari Dutta.

BONKU: And you can't imagine what meeting you has meant to me.

(ANG *leaps back on the top of the machine. The petals now close and* ANG *disappears from view.*

BONKU *watches as the spaceship takes off as smoothly as it had landed, with a sharp whistling sound.*)

CHOWDHURY'S DRAWING ROOM.

Everybody reacts to the whistling sound.

RAMKANAI *rushes to the window and shouts—"Look!" in a voice filled with wonder. The others cluster around him. The light from the spaceship grows smaller and smaller.*

The bamboo grove.

BONKU *is now left alone. He is obviously deeply moved by the experience, and wipes a tear with his dhoti. Then he glances at the tube in his hand, and his face is wreathed in a smile. This grows into a laughter—a laughter of triumph.*

But BONKU *suddenly stops. He seems to make up his mind, and starts walking back the way he came, with firm footsteps.*

CHOWDHURY'S DRAWING ROOM.

BONKU *enters with a flourish.*

BHAIRAB: Look who's here! It's Bunkum!

CHOWDHURY: Hallo, what brings you back?

BONKU: First, let me tell you that my name is not Bunkum. It is Bonkubihari Dutta. Anyone who calls me Bunkum will have his nose rubbed against the wall. I have come to tell you that you were wrong and I was right. A spaceship from another planet in another solar system did land here. Not in London, not in New York, not in Tokyo or Paris or Moscow—but here in Lochanpur.

RAMKANAI: So it was the spaceship we saw taking off!

BONKU: I not only saw the spaceship, but met its occupant, Mr Ang. He has given me a wonderful piece of advice. He said I shouldn't take it lying down when people make fun of me. So I have come to tell you this is my last evening here. I don't care what Mr Chowdhury feels about it, and I certainly don't care for the rest of you who come to lick his boots. Well, goodbye from the only man—I repeat, the only man on Earth—who has talked to a creature from another planet. Goodbye!

(BONKU *strides out of the room.*
CHOWDHURY *stares open-mouthed at the door.*)
Final fade out.

THE ALIEN

Ray in Hollywood. This photograph shot by Cal Montney in 1967 was used by *LA Times* for press coverage of *The Alien*

THE ALIEN:
A TREATMENT

LOCALE: Village Mangalpur in West Bengal
TIME: October 1967

SCENE 1. EXTERIOR. NIGHT. LOTUS POND.

A lotus pond in the village of Mangalpur in West Bengal. The camera holds on a part of the surface of the pond with lotus leaves and limp lotus stalks, lit by soft moonlight.

A point of light appears as a reflection in the water, grows bigger and bigger until the pond itself is lit up. The chorus of frogs, crickets and jackals grows in volume, and is joined by a humming sound. In a blaze of light something descends on the pond, shattering its placidity. A cascade of water descends on the lotus leaves, and the camera tilts up and zooms back to a full shot of the pond.

A dome-like object is seen sinking into the water. The pulsating light that emanates from it dims into total darkness as the object slowly disappears below the surface. As the surface calms down, in the deadly silence that now pervades, all the limp lotus stalks straighten up and open their petals at the same time.

Titles begin over this shot.

SCENE 2. EXTERIOR. DAY. LOTUS POND.

With the last titles, moonlight changes into the light of morning. A song sung casually in a boyish voice is heard—a simple, touching folk ballad about the beauty of flowers and birdsong and fields of grass and paddy. The camera pans to show a bamboo forest by the pond, and in that forest a little boy is collecting twigs, and singing.

SCENE 3. EXTERIOR. DAY. BAMBOO GROVE.

The boy is dressed in rags, and is obviously very poor. In the background, a bent old woman is seen sweeping out dry bamboo leaves from around a shack made of twigs and dry coconut leaves.

The boy HABA *picks up a twig, straightens up, and catches sight of the lotuses in the pond. His singing stops and his mouth falls open. Then he turns to the old woman and shouts:*

"Grandma, come and see the lotuses!"

(GRANDMA *is nearly deaf*)

"What?" she asks.

"The lotuses in the pond," says HABA.

(HABA *now runs over to her and tries to drag her to the pond, but* GRANDMA *flares up.*)

"You know I have lumbago and you want me to go running with you to see this and see that...'

(HABA *has to give up. He drops the twigs and walks away.*)

SCENE 4. EXTERIOR. DAY. THE TEA STALL IN THE MARKETPLACE.

This is the place where the village elders meet in the morning and afternoon to discuss weighty problems and to gossip.

Sitting on hard benches in front of the shop, and sipping tea, are MR BOSE *the advocate,* PRAMANICK *the postmaster and* SARKAR *the homoeopath.*

MR BOSE asks MR SARKAR: "Have you been to see old Mr Narayan this morning?"

"I looked in on my way here."

"How is he?"

"Just as you'd expect him to be, at eighty-seven."

"Well, I hope he doesn't live to see another famine," says BOSE.

"The way the crops are looking..."

"I heard a rumble last night, and felt a chill. For a moment I thought it was rain," says PRAMANICK.

(BOSE *says he had the same feeling.*

In the meantime, HABA *has arrived and has promptly assumed the role of a beggar. He walks up to* BOSE *with outstretched palms.*)

"It's only for a cup of tea, mister," says HABA in a whining falsetto.

"So you've come pestering us again?" barks BOSE. "Off with you, you little rascal!"

(*Then he turns to* MOHAN *who has just arrived.* MOHAN *has the obvious look of a city-bred educated youth.*)

"Good morning," says BOSE. "How's your essay going?"

"What I'm writing doesn't deserve that dignified term, Mr Bose. It's only a series of newspaper articles."

"Well, sit down and tell us about it. We've been watching you talking to people and taking notes."

"Oh, it's about village life, you know."

"But what is there new to write about village life?"

(HABA *is still hanging around, and now sidles up to* MOHAN.)

"I'm hungry mister," he whines. "Haven't had anything to eat since yesterday."

PRAMANICK barks out: "And what about all the fruits you've been stealing from our orchards?"

MOHAN smiles indulgently. "What would you like? Biscuits?"

"And a cup of tea, Babu," says HABA.

(MOHAN *asks the shopkeeper to give the boy tea and biscuits.*)

BOSE says, "Now you've spoilt him for good. He'll make our lives miserable."

MOHAN ignores the remark. He says: "You don't think life in the village has changed much? You may be watching television very shortly, you know."

"But will that help to change the climate at our will? Will it bring rain when we need it? Can we ever get good crops without rains? And can people ever eat and live decently without a good harvest?"

MOHAN says: "Well, science is trying—they are even creating rainfall artificially these days—only on a very small scale of course. But surely a lot is being done to improve irrigation and crops—new methods which haven't been done before."

"Such as the tubewell that's going to come up?" asks SARKAR.

MR BOSE says: "Why they had to get an American to do it, I don't understand."

"He's being employed by an Indian firm," says MOHAN. "It's a new kind of drilling rig which hasn't been used before. He's going to train up local people."

PRAMANICK shakes his head. "We had Americans living around here during the war. Soldiers. And I tell you they were worse than tigers. And what they did to our women…"

MOHAN laughs. "This is no soldier, Mr Pramanick. And I don't think this American will be around longer than three or four days."

Scene 5. Exterior. Day. Sky.
There is a rent in the cloud, and the sun shines through it.

Scene 6. Exterior. Day. Lotus pond.
Sunlight bathes the lotus pond.

Scene 7. Exterior. Day. Cabin of spaceship, inside the capsule.
An oval patch of sunlight forms ripples over the three-fingered hand, and—activates it. The hand slowly moves out of the frame.

Scene 8. Exterior. Day. Underwater view of lotus pond.
Through the round window of the capsule, we get an underwater view of the pond, consisting of fish, lotus stalks and other typical flora and fauna.

A dark form now enters the frame from below, obstructing the view. This is the head of the lone occupant of the spaceship—the ALIEN.

SCENE 9. EXTERIOR. DAY. CABIN OF SPACESHIP.

Now we look in from outside and see the face of the ALIEN: *large head, sunken cheeks, small mouth, nose and ears, sunken eyes with pupils—if they exist at all—lost in the depths of the sockets.*

SCENE 10. INTERIOR. DAY. CABIN OF SPACESHIP.

The ALIEN *moves away from the window.*

With a wave of his hand, the ALIEN *activates a control and the spaceship rises slowly.*

SCENE 11. EXTERIOR. DAY. UNDERWATER VIEW OF POND.

Looking through the window, we see the spaceship slowly surfacing.

SCENE 12. EXTERIOR. DAY. LOTUS POND.

A shot of the pond surface shows the conical, spirelike top of the spaceship coming out of the water. It comes to a stop about two feet above the surface, and stands glistening among the lotuses.

The ALIEN *moves to the viewport again, and from his point of view, we see—*

HABA *standing on the shore, munching a biscuit.*

SCENE 13. EXTERIOR. DAY. CABIN OF SPACESHIP.

Close-up of the ALIEN. *The eyesockets light up—almost imperceptibly—with a green light, which begins to intensify. The* ALIEN *has super vision, and green indicates that he is observing telescopically.*

SCENE 14. INTERIOR. DAY. CABIN OF SPACESHIP.

HABA *is thus brought up very close indeed, and we study, through the eyes of the* ALIEN, *every tiny movement of his facial muscles, his five-fingered hand, and the darting look in his eyes.*

SCENE 15. INTERIOR. DAY. CABIN OF SPACESHIP.

Now the green light in the ALIEN's *eyes dim and disappear, and he moves away from the window to activate another control which immediately brings all the sounds of the outside world into the cabin of the ship. We hear* HABA *singing his favourite song—probably the only one he knows. We also hear bird noises, and the bark of a dog, and another sound which comes, as we shall soon find out, from the drilling site.*

Location hunting in rural Bengal for *The Alien*.
Stills from *The Creative Person: Satyajit Ray*, a documentary by James Beveridge (1967)

All these sounds make distinctive coloured patterns on a screen on the wall of the cabin. The ALIEN *observes these patterns very carefully.*

SCENE 16. EXTERIOR. DAY. DRILLING SITE.

This is less than a quarter of a mile from the pond, and about twenty yards up a slope from the road which connects Mangalpur to the highway a couple of miles away.

The drilling rig is now being set up. DEVLIN, *in charge of the operation, is a brawny, brooding American in his early thirties. He gives the unmistakable impression of being both energetic and dependable. One feels he has a certain reserve of charm and bonhomie which he perhaps uses very sparingly, and is certainly unlikely to overuse in the present circumstances of hard work in a hot, unfamiliar terrain.*

Just now DEVLIN *is having his cigarette lit by* MR GAGANLAL BAJORIA, *a spruce Marwari industrialist in his middle fifties, the proprietor of the firm which has engaged* DEVLIN *and his equipment for the drilling job.*

BAJORIA says: "Well, I think I'll buzz back to the city now. If there's anything more I can do for you…"

"Thanks," says DEVLIN. "This is fine."

"… except that I don't think I can do much about the heat, ha ha."

"Which reminds me," says DEVLIN, who has just spotted a group of young Santhal girls moving along the dusty road, "What's the scene around here—?"

"Scene …?" BAJORIA is puzzled.

"Chicks—broads—" DEVLIN nods towards the Santhal girls.

"Oh chicks!" BAJORIA gets the message. "They are Santhal girls." He goes on confidentially. "Those who consider themselves connoisseurs say they are among the most beautiful women in the world—"

(DEVLIN *watches them and the girls become aware of his look. One of them, a very lovely girl, gives him a long sultry stare and moves on with her companions. As they turn the bend, they are obviously discussing the big American.*)

"Their village is over there"—BAJORIA points—"I'm sure you'll find it without any trouble—they dance quite often when the moon is full…"

"No kiddin'?" says DEVLIN, and then switches to a serious mood, turning towards the site. "Well, if I don't fall off the rig and break my bones or something, I reckon on moving on to the next site tomorrow afternoon."

(MOHAN *has been hovering in the vicinity, now moves up and addresses* BAJORIA.)

"Excuse me, you're Mr Bajoria, aren't you?"

"Yes."

"I represent the *Calcutta Herald*. I'd like to do a little item on this new device that's being—"

"Well, Mr Delvin here knows all about the new device; it's his baby, so—"

"Delvin's what I'm doing. The name's Devlin."

"Oh yes, yes—Devlin, Devlin ... Well—"

"So long—see you tomorrow."

"See you tomorrow. Best of luck!"

DEVLIN turns to MOHAN. "Look, I gotta spud in..."

(*He starts to move towards the rig—*MOHAN *walks with him.*)

"Just a couple of questions, Mr Devlin: what's new about this device?"

"Digs deeper wider quicker." DEVLIN notices HABA in the background salaaming repeatedly and showing his teeth. "Say, you reckon that kid could get me a green coconut?"

MOHAN turns and sees HABA. He asks him in Bengali: "Can you bring the sahib a green coconut?"

(HABA *gives a quick nod and darts off.*)

MOHAN continues: "This is the first rotary rig I've seen with such a small Kelly—"

This obviously raises MOHAN in DEVLIN's estimation, and he says with a smile, "I see you done your homework."

MOHAN smiles. "Water drilling is very important to India's future, Mr Devlin!"

DEVLIN says, "Yeah."

They reach the rig—MOHAN says, "One last question, please. Do you like our country?"

DEVLIN gives a broad toothy smile and says, "Yeah, it's a regular home from home!" He begins to peel off his shirt.

Scene 17. Exterior. Day. Coconut grove.

HABA *climbs dexterously down a coconut tree, picks up the fruit he has dropped from above, and is about to make off for the drilling site, when shouts are heard.*

"Thief! Little scoundrel!"

(HABA *takes to his heels.*

A man—presumably the owner of the tree—picks up a stone and throws it at the boy. The stone hits the boy squarely on the back of the head and makes him stumble forward.

MOHAN, *on his way back from the drilling site, watches this and runs up to* HABA. *The boy gets up on his feet, rubbing the back of his head with his free hand, which gets blood on it.*

The owner comes charging up from behind. But HABA *runs off.*)

"Why did you let the boy go?" asks the irate owner.

"Was that your coconut?"

"Yes—and I'm going to turn that boy over to the cops one of these days."

"How much did the coconut cost?" asks MOHAN, bringing out his purse.

The man simmers down. "It's not that," he says. "You don't have to pay. But you mustn't encourage that boy. He's a born thief."

(MOHAN *looks at the departing* HABA.)

SCENE 18. EXTERIOR. DAY. DRILLING SITE.

HABA comes charging up the slope. "Salaam, sahib, salaam."

DEVLIN walks over. "Thanks!" He hands the boy a shining eight anna bit and collects the green coconut.

SINGH, DEVLIN's assistant, walks over and says, "Shall I cut it for you, chief?"

SCENE 19. INTERIOR. DAY. CABIN OF SPACESHIP.

The windows of the capsule.

The ALIEN *is still looking out.*

SCENE 20. EXTERIOR. DAY. LOTUS POND.

HABA *comes back from the drilling site. He flicks the coin up in the air and holds it as it drops. Then he feels his wound again. It is still bleeding.*

SCENE 21. INTERIOR. DAY. CABIN OF SPACESHIP.

The ALIEN's *eyes turn green and he sees the blood in close-up.*

SCENE 22. EXTERIOR. DAY. LOTUS POND.

Then he sees the wound when HABA *bends over to wash his hand in the pond.*

SCENE 23. INTERIOR. DAY. CABIN OF SPACESHIP.

Now a new thumping sound suddenly invades the capsule. The ALIEN's *eyelights dim and he turns to the screen. A new, bold sound pattern, sharply rhythmic, forms on the screen.*

Scene 24. Exterior. Day. Drilling site.

The drill has started to operate, and its ponderous rhythmic thud now fills the countryside.

Scene 25. Interior. Evening. Bedroom of Narayan.

NARAYAN's *bedroom. Eighty-seven-year-old* NARAYAN, *the oldest inhabitant of Mangalpur, lies seriously ill.* DR SARKAR *is feeling his pulse. Gathered round his bed are members of* NARAYAN's *family: his grandson and his wife, and their two small children.*

We also see MR BOSE, PRAMANICK *and another middle-aged man near the door.*

DR SARKAR *gets up and walks towards the door, speaking to the grandson in a low voice:*

"He might last through this night, but tomorrow being a full moon…"

Scene 26. Exterior. Night. Narayan's house.

The visitors come out of the house. BOSE *turns to* PRAMANICK *and says:*

"It's the food they ate in those golden days—no adulteration, you know—which has given them such stamina. Milk one anna per seer—can you imagine?"

"I know," says PRAMANICK. "My father lived to be ninety-two!"

Scene 27. Exterior. Night. Drilling site.

DEVLIN *comes out of his tent. A breeze is blowing.* DEVLIN *draws in a deep breath. Soft moonlight bathes the gaunt form of the drilling rig.* DEVLIN *takes out his whisky flask from his pocket and drinks. The words of a ballad form on his lips, and he hums.*

Now he reacts to a sound of drumming: tribal drums of the Santhals. It comes from a village diagonally across the paddy.

DEVLIN *starts to walk in that direction.*

Scene 28. Exterior. Night. Bo tree by the temple.

He has to walk past the Bo tree beside the Kali temple. Below the tree sits a sadhu with a beard and matted hair. By his side are disciples one of whom is preparing a chillum of ganja. DEVLIN *slows down to take a better look, then resumes his normal gait.*

Scene 29.

He walks past the temple now, where a puja is in progress. Two young women come out of the temple and walk up in the direction of DEVLIN. *At the sight of him, they stop, turn around, and scamper off, drawing their saris across their faces.* DEVLIN *raises his eyebrows, shrugs and continues to walk, humming the ballad in snatches.*

SCENE 30. INTERIOR. NIGHT. MOHAN'S BEDROOM.

MOHAN *is glancing through the day's newspaper before getting down to resuming his article.* MOHAN's *newly-married wife* KALYANI *comes in plaiting her hair.*

A girl of about 19, KALYANI *has a soft, gentle beauty which is yet capable of unexpected animation. She stands with her back to the window and looking at her husband.*

KALYANI says, "I wish you were doing a series on the mountains. Then we could go up to Darjeeling. That would be a real honeymoon."

MOHAN keeps his eyes on the newspaper page and says, "Did you see a moving light in the sky last night?"

"What moving light?"

"They say some observers in West Bengal have seen it."

(KALYANI *regards him gravely.* MOHAN *throws the newspaper aside.*)

Then she sighs and says, "I didn't say anything would move here, really. Or anything would happen. I wonder..."

"Strange," he says.

"What's strange?"

"You and I sitting and talking here in this sleepy hole, while they are getting ready to land the first men on the moon. Can you imagine what that means, Kalyani?"

(*She moves up near the bed behind him and runs her fingers softly down his neck.*)

"I know what it doesn't mean. It doesn't mean better prospects for you, because they won't send you to the moon to report on the landing!"

(MOHAN *gets up and starts pacing the floor with excitement.*)

"But just think—for the first time in the history of mankind—which means the first time in a million years—man will set foot on the moon!"

"And will they find the old woman at the spinning wheel, I wonder."

(KALYANI *has moved up to the window again and is looking out at the moon.*)

MOHAN says, "I'm afraid the old woman will be where she's always been—in the nursery rhymes."

(MOHAN suddenly slumps down on the bed in apparent despair.)

"It's unfair," he says bitterly.

"Unfair?"

"You know who discovered the zero?"

"Zero? What are you talking about?" KALYANI is really puzzled.

"One-two-three-four-five-six-seven-eight-nine—zero. You put a zero after one and it becomes one more than nine. Every zero makes ten times more. Isn't that

Ray and his unit interacting with local people while scouting for locations

wonderful! We discovered that zero—an unknown Indian—way back in the time of the Upanishads."

(KALYANI keeps intently looking on.)

"And that changed the course of history—by changing the course of mathematics. But then—then we lost ground."

(MOHAN *sighs. He walks over to the window, puts his arms around* KALYANI, *and looks up at the sky.*)

KALYANI says, "When are we going to finish here and get back to the city?"

"Very soon—and you can make it sooner, Kalyani."

"How?"

"I've been talking to the men. I want you to talk to the women."

"Talk about what?"

"Ask them what they think about family planning." KALYANI's mouth falls open. "Ask them if they use what they're told to use…"

(KALYANI *moves forward and clamps her hand over* MOHAN's *mouth.* MOHAN *embraces her.*)

"Now what if they ask me?"

"Tell them the truth," says MOHAN.

(*The two go into another embrace.*)

"*Shunya*—it means space, and it means zero—both. Isn't that wonderful?"

"Wonderful," says KALYANI.

(*She leans back and he buries his face in the perfume of her long black hair.*)

Scene 31. Exterior. Night. Santhal village.

The dance has reached a peak of frenzy. The girls, about twenty of them, have interlocked their arms and have formed a semicircle. They step backwards and forwards to the music in a gentle undulating movement. The men play the drums and flutes. DEVLIN *sits on a mound a little way away, drinking the local wine from a day pot. His feet keep tapping to the beat of the music. The girls are oblivious of their surroundings, dancing, singing, and laughing, their silver ornaments glinting in the moonlight.* DEVLIN *finishes the drink and throws the pot away. Then he gets up and saunters up close to the dancers. He walks round behind the girls, appraising them with a connoisseur's eye. Unerringly he selects the prettiest girl and takes a position behind her so that she almost touches him at the end of each backward movement.*

DEVLIN *starts watching the movement of the girl's body, the bare shoulders, the nape of the neck, the way the plaited hair has been knotted into a bun. Now he puts out his hand and pulls out a silver ornament from the girl's hair. The girl doesn't notice it.* DEVLIN *twirls the ornament in his hand for a few seconds, then pushes it back into place as the girl gets close again. Then he moves up to the drummer and watches him for a while, and saunters away.*

SCENE 32. INTERIOR. NIGHT. REV. BISWAS'S COTTAGE.

The padre, REV. BISWAS, *lives in a cottage by the side of the modest little church. He is seen fixing his mosquito curtain in his bedroom. He reacts, glancing up at the window. Then he hurries out of the room and out of the cottage, and comes up to the wicket.*

SCENE ·33. EXTERIOR. NIGHT. REV. BISWAS'S COTTAGE AND CHURCH.

DEVLIN *stands outside, cigarette in mouth, clicking away at his lighter which doesn't seem to work.*

"Good evening," says REV. BISWAS.

DEVLIN looks up at the padre and says, "Evening. You have a light? I've run out of gas!"

"Light? Light?"

(*The padre is flustered. He runs back into his room and comes out with a lighted candle, guarding the flame carefully with his free hand.* DEVLIN *lights his cigarette.*)

"Thanks. This your church?"

(*The padre smiles and nods.*)

"Who comes to pray?" asks DEVLIN, walking in through the wicket a few steps towards the church.

"I have my little—flock … the Santhals…" Padre points in the direction of the music.

"The what?"

"Santhals. The tribals."

"They Christians?" surprise in DEVLIN's voice.

"Some of them, not all," says the padre. "You see, they are the aboriginals of India, and they have no conception of God or divinity."

"You converted them?"

(*The padre shrugs.*)

"There were others before me, too … It's not an easy task."

(DEVLIN *glances in the direction of the music.* BISWAS *is embarrassed.*)

"Those that come to church, they sing hymns…"

"You don't like this kind of music?"

(The padre doesn't know what else to say. He suspects the American likes it. There is a moment's awkward silence. Then DEVLIN *smiles and says)*

"Well, thanks for the light," and walks away.

(The padre looks on, holding the candle in his hand. The words of a ballad come floating to him, making a strange counterpoint to the tribal music.)

> "If you're travelin' in the north country fair
>
> Where the wind hits heavy on the borderline
>
> Remember me to one who lives there
>
> She was once a true love of mine..."

SCENE 34. INTERIOR. NIGHT. CABIN OF SPACESHIP.

Inside the capside. On the screen—delicate patterns formed by the shrilling of crickets and the croaking of frogs. The Santhal music is a component too.

Now another sound is added: DEVLIN *is singing.*

> "I'm wondering if she remembers me at all...
>
> Many times I've hoped and prayed
>
> In the darkness of my night
>
> In the brightness of my days..."

(The voice fades out.

The ALIEN *moves his hand and activates another control.)*

SCENE 35. EXTERIOR. NIGHT. LOTUS POND.

A shot of the exterior of the spaceship shows its top opening like a lid.

Through the opening the ALIEN *comes out. The* ALIEN *is a cross between a gnome and a famished refugee child. Large head, spindly limbs, a lean torso. Is he male, female or neuter? We don't know. What his form basically conveys is a kind of ethereal innocence, and it is difficult to associate either great power or great evil with him. And yet a feeling of eerieness is there because of the resemblance to a sickly human child. The* ALIEN *stands poised on the top of the spaceship for a few seconds, then takes a leap and lands gently, almost weightlessly, on a lotus leaf.*

He looks down on the surface of the water, gets down on his knees, touches the water with his finger. Then he examines the water very closely. Blue lights appear in the sockets of his eyes, enabling the water to be observed microscopically.

Ray with his cinematographer Subrata Mitra

SCENE 36. MICROSCOPIC DETAIL.

Germs, amoeba and other minute forms of life are revealed to the ALIEN. *We can even hear the sound they make while they swim.*

SCENE 37. EXTERIOR. NIGHT. LOTUS POND.

Now the lights in his eyes dim, and the ALIEN *stands up. There is a certain tension about him, as if he had to be watchful of traps. Then suddenly, in a series of fantastically quick, short steps over the lotus leaves, the* ALIEN *reaches the shore of the pond. He looks down at the grass, examines a blade, and is off hopping into the bamboo forest.*

SCENE 38. EXTERIOR. NIGHT. BAMBOO GROVE.

There the ALIEN *sees a small plant. He passes his hand over it, and flowers come out. A thin soft high-pitched laugh shows the* ALIEN *is pleased. He plucks a flower, puts it into his mouth, and hops on all fours to an anthill. He pokes the anthill with his finger and causes agitated ants to swarm out of their holes. The* ALIEN *observes the ants with his microscopic vision, and attunes his ears to make audible the sounds made by the insects.*

Looking up, the ALIEN *laughs to see a swarm of fireflies dancing around a mango tree. He leaps up, catches hold of a mango branch and keeps swinging, while the fireflies dance around him.*

SCENE 39. EXTERIOR. NIGHT. HABA'S SHACK.

Poised in mid-air, the ALIEN *sees* HABA's *shack. He goes flitting through the air to reach the door of the shack to see* HABA *huddled in sleep on a mat.*

The ALIEN's *eyelights now turn a glowing red which enables him to see* HABA's *respiratory system and listen to his regular heartbeats. The red in the* ALIEN's *eyes now turns violet and he looks into* HABA's *brain and sinks into his subconscious.*

SCENE 40. HABA'S DREAMLAND.

HABA *is dreaming, and the* ALIEN *becomes part of his dream. We see* HABA *and the* ALIEN *playing hide-and-seek in a strange black-and-white world of geometrical forms.*

SCENE 41. EXTERIOR. NIGHT. HABA'S SHACK.

The light in the ALIEN's *eyes now dim, and with another high-pitched laugh, he is gone from the bamboo forest.*

SCENE 42. EXTERIOR. NIGHT. PADDY FIELD.

The ALIEN *now comes to the paddy field and sees the withering crop. He examines a paddy plant. His eyes turn yellow, and he dances about in the field while all the paddy around him ripens and stands aspiring in the moonlight. Standing on the tip of a paddy plant, the* ALIEN *looks up at the sky.*

SCENE 43. EXTERIOR. NIGHT. SKY.

The moon fascinates him. He turns on his green eyelights and brings the moon close for inspection.

SCENE 44.

Then the ALIEN *pushes the moon back in place, jumps off the paddy, and flits back to the spaceship.*

Fade out.

SCENE 45. EXTERIOR. DAY. GOVINDA'S HUT.

GOVINDA, *the peasant, comes out of his hut, rubbing his eyes and yawning. He pats his cattle, yawns again, and ambles towards his field.*

SCENE 46. EXTERIOR. DAY. PADDY FIELD.

The sight that meets his eyes makes his mouth fall open. A slow-witted man, GOVINDA *can only scratch his head, walk over to examine the crop, walk back again, shake his head and scratch it again.*

In a while, the news begins to spread and the whole village gathers at the field to see the strange sight.

BHATTACHARJI, the priest declares, "This is indeed a miracle. All praise to Mother Annapurna."

(*Some people make obeisance to the paddy.*)

MR BOSE, shrewder than the others, says, "You know, we shouldn't discount the possibility of that American having done something with some new fertilizer or other..."

(BOSE's *suggestion meets with scant approval.*

MOHAN *is among those present. He looks tense, having smelled a story. He takes the still-bemused* GOVINDA *aside and says*)

"How do you feel about this strange occurrence, Govinda?"

"How do I feel?" GOVINDA shakes his head. "I ask you, mister, how you would feel if you had a one-year-old child—a sickly child, to be sure—but whom you gave all your love and care, and suddenly one morning you found him a full grown man. How would you feel then, mister?"

(MOHAN *takes rapid notes in his pad, but is distracted by* HABA's *shouting.*)

"Come and see the new temple, the new temple!"

"What new temple?" someone asks.

"The new temple in the lotus pond," says Haba. "And I found this mango too."

(HABA *holds up a luscious green mango for everyone to see.*)

"Mango in October?" Everybody is astounded.

(HABA *has already started running in the direction of the lotus pond, and the crowd turns to follow* HABA.)

SCENE 47. INTERIOR. DAY. CABIN OF SPECESHIP.

A babble of human voices invades the cabin and makes strange new sound patterns on the screen. The ALIEN *looks through the crystalline viewport and watches the crowd arriving.*

SCENE 48. EXTERIOR. DAY. LOTUS POND.

HABA *points triumphantly to the shining top of the spaceship and says,*

"There it is."

(*All eyes go to the spaceship.*)

Now HABA says, "My friend is in that temple, and he is the one who has made all the fruits and the flowers to grow."

(*He is promptly knuckled on the head for saying so.*)

"My friend is in there, indeed!" growls BHATTACHARJI, aiming another clout at the boy. "Don't you start showing off again, my lad, this is a religious matter and if you talk like that you'll get the thrashing of your life!"

(*But* MOHAN *has been watching* HABA. *He draws the boy aside and says:*)

"What friend have you got in there, Haba?"

"It's a little boy like me," says HABA, a trifle deflated. "He came down from the stars."

"I see. And how did you know that?"

"He told me," says HABA. "He was in my dream last night."

"Oh, I see. Very good," says MOHAN, both playing up to him and dismissing him at the same time.

"And he's healed my wound too," says HABA, rubbing his head.

(*But* MOHAN's *attention has strayed to the spaceship, and he keeps looking at it with a puzzled expression. Then, somewhat unexpectedly, he picks up a stone and throws it at the spaceship. It hits the object and makes a metallic sound.*

The elders in the crowd turn menacingly at MOHAN.)

"That was a very foolish thing to do, young man," says BOSE, hissing out each syllable.

(MOHAN *manages to keep his composure and says*)

"I was only trying to see if it was metal. It could have been a stage-prop, you know, made of pith or wood or something."

(*Others join* BOSE *now in accusing* MOHAN *of having risked sacrilege, and all that* MOHAN *can do is to withdraw into the shade of a tree, and marvel at the rapidity with which the idea of the temple, and the attribution of the miracle to the temple, gains ground.*)

Scene 49. Interior. Day. Cabin of spaceship.

Inside the capsule, the ALIEN *has been watching everything in close-up with his super vision. His eyes dim, and he turns away from the window. Then he starts to hop about the cabin in what is obviously a state of great excitement.*

Scene 50. Exterior. Day. Drilling site.

A man from the village runs up the slope and whispers the news of the temple to one of the workers. The news begins to spread.

DEVLIN, *climbing down from the rig, notices the buzz of conversation, and shouts.*

"Okay, break it up, what's going on here?"

(*One man had moved away from his position.* DEVLIN *glowers at him.*)

"Where the hell ya think ya goin'? Get back on the job!"

(*The man reluctantly resumes his position.*

SINGH *draws up beside* DEVLIN, *who stands cleaning the black grease from his hands with a piece of waste.*)

SINGH says, "A very strange thing has happened, chief. A temple has—"

"Aw, get outa here!" says DEVLIN, walking away to meet BAJORIA, who had watched the sudden explosion of temper and had been waiting for a lull to greet the American.

"Morning, Jim," he says. "You don't mind my calling you Jim?"

"Nope! 'Cept that my parents called me Joe," says DEVLIN, bringing out his packet of cigarettes.

"Oh, sorry, I thought the J stood for—"

"That's okay! How're you this morning?"

"Well, fine." BAJORIA lights DEVLIN's cigarette and hands him the lighter. "It was easier to get a gas lighter than just gas."

"Oh!" says DEVLIN, surprised and touched. "Say, thanks!"

"A pleasure. How's it going?"

"Great. See the water?"

"So your hunch paid off!"

"Usually does." DEVLIN looks at the sun. "On schedule. Stay for lunch?"

"I'll stick around a bit if I won't be in the way—"

"No—'s all right, I'll be right back."

(DEVLIN *strides off to attend to some unfinished business.* BAJORIA *calls* SINGH, *who comes over quickly.*)

"What was the trouble, Singh?" asks BAJORIA.

"No trouble, sir. Just something which has happened in that village over there. They say a temple has come out of a pond…"

"A temple?"

"Yes, sir."

"Out of a pond?"

"Yes, sir."

SCENE 51. EXTERIOR. DAY. LOTUS POND.

KALYANI *looks around for her husband. She spots him in the shade of a clump of bamboos and walks over.*

MOHAN *looks up at* KALYANI, *who is obviously piqued.*

"You might at least have come home and told me," she says.

"Sit down, Kalyani," says MOHAN.

(*We see a group of women clustered on the opposite bank. Some are making obeisance. Some throw flowers into the water. The conversation is hushed, and there is already an air of religious awe pervading the place.*

KALYANI *sits down beside her husband.* MOHAN's *pad and pencil lie on the grass beside him.*)

"I thought I'd find you happy and working, and now I find you worried and—"

"It's upset all my calculations, Kalyani," says MOHAN.

(KALYANI *keeps silent. She already knows her husband's moods.*)

"When it first happened, I thought, My God, what a story! But now…"

(KALYANI *waits for further revelation.*)

MOHAN says, "You know, I don't think I could ever make a good reporter. A reporter mustn't think for himself. He should just write what he sees and what he hears. He should be a conveyor belt, no more. But I can't help thinking. I can't help asking myself why such a thing should happen in the twentieth century, and I can't find an answer. How can I write? It's the answer I want to write about, and I can't find it."

(*The sound of a car breaks the spell, and both* KALYANI *and* MOHAN *rise to their feet.*

BAJORIA's *Impala arrives in a cloud of dust and pulls up by the lotus pond.* MOHAN *rises, his eyes narrowing—he ignores* KALYANI.)

KALYANI says, "Don't tell me you won't be home for lunch again!"

MOHAN says, "I'll come when I'm hungry."

(*After a long look,* KALYANI *goes away.*

BAJORIA *has got out of the car, and stands gazing at the spaceship. Inside the spaceship, the* ALIEN *observes* BAJORIA *and the Impala.* BAJORIA *has spotted* MOHAN *and nods a friendly greeting.* MOHAN *moves up to him.*)

"Aren't you the reporter chap I met yesterday?"

(MOHAN *nods.*)

BAJORIA, "There must be a good story for you there."

(MOHAN *smiles.*)

"You belong here?"

"No. Calcutta."

"What is this village called?"

"Mangalpur."

"Aha—the land of well-being—great name."

(*He turns to the crowd and says in Bengali*)

"Apnader gramer naam khub bhalo achche." (Your village has a fine name.)

(*Turning to* MOHAN *again*)

"Well, ever seen a temple like that before?"

"Never."

"Must be the only one of its kind. I've made quite a study of temples. You know, I've beeen restoring ruined temples all over India."

"I do, Mr Bajoria."

"Are you in favour of such restoration or not? Be frank with me. I won't put you in jail if you say no."

"Then I have to say no."

"Why not?"

"I feel works of art should be left alone."

"Even crumbling-down ones? Even when they are also places of worship? What happens in fifty years then? We have no works of art and no places of worship. Don't you see? At least I'm giving religion a new lease of life."

"I'm sure you have God himself on your side, Mr Bajoria."

"I do. I really think I do. That temple there tells me so. It was God's own design that it should come out so near my drilling site."

"And how do you think it got there, Mr Bajoria?"

"Very simple. It has always been there, below the pond. Maybe below the soil. Maybe for ten thousand years. It's the explosives they've used there that's pushed it up to the surface."

(BAJORIA *starts humming—*)

Scene 52. Interior. Day. Cabin of spaceship.

To the ALIEN, BAJORIA *is now an X-ray photograph.*

Scene 53. Exterior. Day. Lotus pond.

Bajoria stops humming and says, "I haven't the slightest doubt that Mangalpur is going to be the greatest place of pilgrimage in India—very soon."

(*A sudden soft, somewhat shrill laugh greets this announcement.* BAJORIA *turns around.*)

"Who was that?" he asks grimly.

(*The people look at one another, puzzled. Even* MOHAN *is a little puzzled.*)

"Silly fools!" says BAJORIA, getting into his car.

(*He beckons to* MOHAN, *who walks over.* BAJORIA *says in a low voice*)

"You want to make good—make a mark as a reporter, don't you?"

"Naturally!"

"I hope you won't do any rash reporting on this. Wait 'til tomorrow, young man, and I'll give you an exclusive story that'll make the headlines in every paper you can think of—left, right, front, back or middle—understand?"

"You're very kind!"

(MOHAN's *sarcasm is lost on* BAJORIA *who has already wound up his window.*)

SCENE 54. EXTERIOR. DAY. DRILLING SITE.

DEVLIN *seems in a good mood and rubs his hands.*

"Singh!" he calls out.

(SINGH *runs up.*)

"Pull it down, we'll eat lunch now. Tell the crew they can go take a look at that pagoda."

SINGH smiles. "I want to go too, chief."

"Okay, but back at two o'clock sharp."

"Okay, chief."

(BAJORIA *arrives.*)

"It's an auspicious day, it seems," he says.

"Come and have a cold beer," says DEVLIN, walking towards the air-conditioned trailer. BAJORIA follows.

SCENE 55. INTERIOR. DAY. TRAILER.

The two men enter. BAJORIA *sits down. He is humming a bhajan.* DEVLIN *gets the drinks and sits facing* BAJORIA.

DEVLIN says, "Happy?"

BAJORIA says, "Yes, Mr Devlin, and I have a proposition."

(DEVLIN *takes a sidelong glance at* BAJORIA, *then pours out the beer. They clink glasses and drink.*)

"Proposition?" says DEVLIN.

(BAJORIA *nods.*)

"You see, there's a pond in that village out there," he says, and in that pond there's a temple. Its top is sticking out of the water."

"Uh-huh."

"I want that pumped out. The water, I mean." A pause.

"Why?" asks DEVLIN.

"Well, *if* it's a temple—and it's most likely to be one, because its coming out has coincided with all sorts of remarkable supernatural happenings—"

"*You* believe in all that crap?"

"But there's no other explanation, Joe. These things don't happen without good reason."

"Oh, come on now—this is—this is crazy."

"There are more things in this blessed country, Mr Devlin, than are dreamt of in *your* philosophy."

"Philosophy's got nuthin' to do with it, Charlie—I'm a driller. You get me out here all the way from Butte, Montana, to bring in water and now you're talking about temples and miracles and ... oh boy!" He drinks.

"Didn't you know that business and religion make the most wonderful cocktail in the world? The most effective, the most miraculous, the most extraordinary mixture in the world."

(DEVLIN *regards* BAJORIA *with a new interest, not unmixed with a certain admiration.*)

He says, "Yeah, maybe you gotta point at that!" He reaches across and takes BAJORIA's hand, examining the large diamond and expensive gold wristwatch that he wears. "Can't say you done too badly if that's how you done it."

(BAJORIA *rubs his hands and the diamonds in his rings flash.*)

"What I've done so far," says BAJORIA, "is nothing. Nuth-thing at all. I want you—"

"Me?"

"Yes, Mr Devlin, you. I want you to pump that water out so that I can cover the floor of that pond with marble, white marble, and build white marble steps leading down from all four sides, and arches and pillars, all white marble, and a little black marble plaque with gold letters to say: Salvaged and Restored by Gaganlal Bajoria. That village out there, Joe, is going to be one of the holiest places in India."

"But what I don't get is—why pick on me? All you need is a salvage pump—"

"I'll get that."

"Okay—and get an Indian to do the dredging job, while we move on to the next drilling site. You got fine workers here. You don't need me."

"I do, Mr Joe, or I wouldn't have come to you. I am *not* a man of whims. I'm a very level-headed, logical-minded man who weighs everything very carefully before he decides on a course of action."

(BAJORIA *pauses for effect.*)

"I'm listening," says DEVLIN.

Then BAJORIA leans forward, drops his voice to a whisper and says, "Do you have a gun?"

(DEVLIN *stiffens.*)

"What d' you need a gun for?"

"I don't need it—*arre baapre* you do—do you have one?"

"Yeah, I got one."

"Let me see it."

"Now hold on for a minute—you want a shooter, get yourself another boy—I don't want trouble."

"What trouble do you anticipate, Joe? And from whom? You think I don't pull any weight in this country? And what makes you think you'll have to *use* the gun? All I want is that you should have it with you, so that people can see it's there. Just in case."

"In case o' what?"

(BAJORIA *smiles at* DEVLIN.)

"In case of 'what'?"

"You have this temple in the pond—okay?"

"Yeah."

"A very holy temple—yeah? Now, I, Gaganlal Bajoria, want the water pumped out because I want a real solid temple where people can walk in and worship. My motive—to be truthful—is purely religious. But suppose—just suppose—that the villagers get it into their heads that I'm after that gold."

"What gold?"

"Oh, sorry—forgot to tell you—the temple is covered with gold."

"You don't say!"

"I do say. I'm ninety-five per cent certain it's gold and the thing is—they may have the same suspicion too."

"So you want me with a gun so they don't string you up on that mango tree—is that it?"

"You know how riots start here? You know how the Indian Mutiny started? You'll be surprised. Out of nothing! Nuth-thing! The moment they smell something like that, they'll go for their hammers and sickles, and before you can say Rajagopalachari, I'm a dead man. A dead man, Joe. A bloody corpse."

"Yeah. Saint Bajoria!" DEVLIN gets up on his feet. "You know, Gug," he says, "I have a good mind to grab the next plane back home and to hell with the drilling."

"*Arre, arre*—this is terrible, Joe—I don't know why you take this attitude, really.

This is no crime I'm asking you to do. They pump out the water—the Indians do it. You just stand by with the gun—*buss*! Nuth-thing more! This is no crime. After all, even the US President makes you do certain things you don't like to do."

"Yeah, and we vote him out of office."

(BAJORIA *puts his hand in his coat pocket.*)

"But," says BAJORIA, "votes can be bought, can't they, like candy. You have a family, Joe?"

"No."

"A girlfriend, maybe. A sweetheart, a chick?"

"What you drivin' at now?"

(BAJORIA *brings out his cheque book.*)

"I want to offer you a little Xmas gift, Joe. I'm a bit ahead of time, but then, you won't be here for Xmas!"

(DEVLIN *keeps staring fixedly at* BAJORIA, *his jaws working at the sandwich he has just taken out of a box. He pushes the box towards* BAJORIA, *who has now brought out his pen—a gold Parker.*)

"You have nothing to lose, Joe. And I'm sure it doesn't bother you that you might arouse the wrath of an unknown Hindu deity—possibly with four arms and fourteen legs?"

(DEVLIN *keeps on munching.*)

"And if you're worried about your image, Joe, let me tell you, Americans are widely known to indulge in a lot of strange activities, right here in India, just for the heck of it ... far stranger than pumping water out of a pond—ha, ha!"

(BAJORIA *is about to write out a cheque when* DEVLIN *casually lets the pen out of his hand.* DEVLIN *speaks at last.*)

"Ever get bit by a coyote?"

"Coyote?"

"I once knew a guy who had a coyote bite him when he was a kid. He had the same kinda ... same kinda..."

(DEVLIN *tries to draw patterns in the air to indicate the kind of mind* BAJORIA *has got.*)

SCENE 56. EXTERIOR. NIGHT.

It is a clear sky and the full moon has just risen.

SCENE 57. INTERIOR. NIGHT. NARAYAN'S BEDROOM.

The moonlight comes in through the barred window and falls on the dying NARAYAN'S *face. The old man is now in a state of coma. There are six or seven people in the room, all looking on silently and waiting for the end.*

Suddenly the people in the room react, leaning forward.

NARAYAN *has opened his eyes.*

His eyeballs turn towards the window.

SCENE 58. EXTERIOR. NIGHT. SKY.

We see the starry sky from NARAYAN'S *viewpoint.*

SCENE 59. INTERIOR. NIGHT. NARAYAN'S BEDROOM.

Now NARAYAN *lifts his emaciated right hand. With great effort, he straightens his forefinger and points to the sky.*

His lips begin to work in an effort to form a word.

His son bends over him.

"Do you wish to say something, Father?"

(NARAYAN'S *voice seems to come from a great distance.*)

"A–Ava-Avatar!" he says.

(*The hand drops down.* NARAYAN *is dead.*)

SCENE 60. EXTERIOR. NIGHT. CHURCH.

The cross over the church seen against the full moon.

SCENE 61. INTERIOR. NIGHT. CHURCH.

The padre, REV. BISWAS, *is holding a special service for his small congregation.*

The sermon, of which we hear the concluding words, relates to the miracles, which are cited as instances of the mysterious powers of the Lord.

SCENE 62. EXTERIOR. NIGHT. KALI TEMPLE.

The symbol on the spire of the Hindu temple seen against the full moon.

BHATTACHARJI, *the priest, is conducting a religious ceremony in the temple to the beat of gongs and cymbals and blowing of conchshells.*

SCENE 63. EXTERIOR. NIGHT. SPACESHIP.

The spire of the spaceship seen against the full moon.

SCENE 64. INTERIOR. NIGHT. CABIN OF SPACESHIP.

Inside the spaceship the ALIEN *is looking through the viewport.*

SCENE 65. EXTERIOR. NIGHT. BAMBOO GROVE.

From his point of view, HABA *is seen prowling about in the bamboo forest. Zoom in to a close-up, and he is seen catching a frog and putting it into a sack. Now he moves and is seen to approach a group of fireflies.*

SCENE 66. EXTERIOR. NIGHT. SANTHAL VILLAGE.

DEVLIN *walks into the square where the dancers had been the previous evening. It puzzles him to see that tonight the place is deserted. Even the huts around seem to be empty. A lone pariah dog barks at him; he walks around aimlessly for a while, then goes off towards the church.*

SCENE 67. EXTERIOR. NIGHT. CHURCH.

REV. BISWAS *is pacing about in the moonlight outside his cottage, sees* DEVLIN, *greets him.*

"Good evening."

DEVLIN nods. "Hi, Reverend." He looks around. "Feels kinda spooky tonight. Where's everybody?"

"You mean the dancers?" The padre smiles. "They've gone to a fair ten miles away, in another village."

"H'm."

(*The padre seems tense and anxious to talk.*)

"Er, mister—"

"Devlin's the name."

"Mr Devlin—you're an American, aren't you?"

"Yeah."

"An engineer?"

"Yeah."

"Do you mind if I ask you a question?"

"'Pends on the question!" says DEVLIN with a smile.

"What do you think of miracles?"

(DEVLIN *replies after a brief pause.*)

"I don't think!" he says.

"Don't think what?"

"Don't think. Period." DEVLIN has brought out his whisky flask.

"Do you believe science is the answer to everything?" asks the padre.

"No more 'n this—" says DEVLIN, holding up the flask. He offers it to the padre. "Care for a drink?"

(*The padre smiles and shakes his head.*)

"I've spent seventeen years trying to cure my congregation of the habit."

"If you can't lick 'em, join 'em."

"Pardon?" The padre is not too well up on slang.

DEVLIN smiles and says, "Nuthin'. I'd figured on getting one of those drums to take back with me."

"I'll arrange to send you one," says the padre.

(*From the village of Mangalpur across the paddy fields comes the sound of a funeral chorus.*)

"What's that?" says DEVLIN.

"Somebody died and they're carrying the dead body to the burning ghat."

(DEVLIN *turns to go.*)

Scene 68. Exterior. Night. Lotus pond.

NARAYAN's *bier carried on the shoulders of six persons, with three or four others following in the rear, moves past the pond.*

Scene 69. Interior. Night. Spaceship.

In the capsule, the ALIEN *reacts to the sound and goes to the viewport. His eyes turn green.*

Scene 70. Exterior. Night. Lotus pond.

The ALIEN *sees, in big close-up, the upturned profile of the corpse lying on the bier.*

Scene 71. Exterior. Night. Burning ghat.

DEVLIN *walks past the burning ghat and sees the dead body of* NARAYAN *arriving.*

Scene 72. Exterior. Night. Bo tree.

He walks on and reaches the Bo tree where the sadhu sits with his two disciples. The chillum is being passed round.

DEVLIN *stops to look, then steps forward. The sadhu turns a reddening but not unfriendly eye towards him.* DEVLIN *settles himself on top of an uneven block of stone, the remnant of an old pillar. He looks on for a few seconds at the old mendicant.*

"You a sadhu?" he asks.

(*The sadhu smiles and moves his head in the faintest suggestion of a nod.*)

"What's that mean—a junkie? A pot addict?"

(*The sadhu takes the chillum and has a good pull.* DEVLIN *extends the whisky flask towards the sadhu.*)

"Ya wanna trade vices? This is whisky! Good."

(*Sadhu takes the flask.* DEVLIN *keeps his hand stretched out for the chillum, which only comes after the sadhu has downed the liquor in one mighty gulp.*

DEVLIN *has trouble with the grip.*)

"Hey, how d'you hold this damn thing?"

(*One of the chelas demonstrates.*)

DEVLIN, "Aha!"

(*This time* DEVLIN *gets it right. He puts his mouth to the opening and pulls.*)

Scene 73. Exterior. Night. Burning ghat.

NARAYAN'*s dead body on the funeral pyre.* NARAYAN'*s grandson places a log of wood on the corpse for the cremation.*

From behind an Akanda bush, the ALIEN *watches. His eyes turn red.*

NARAYAN'*s dead body from the* ALIEN'*s point of view. We see the dead man's respiratory system. No movement, no heartbeat.*

The ALIEN'*s eyes. They turn from red to an intense white.* NARAYAN'*s respiratory system. Now there is a return of movement, and the first heartbeat is heard. Then a second.*

One of the pallbearers leans over the body to place a log on it. The face of the corpse.

The eyelids move slowly apart. The lips part. The pallbearer drops the log and starts shaking. A hoarse scream comes out of his mouth.

"My God—he's alive!"

(*He bolts. Others react, bolt, and there is general panic. Another pallbearer, with a sceptical turn of mind, walks up to the corpse. The* ALIEN'*s eyes dim. Pallbearer looks down at the corpse.* NARAYAN *is as dead as ever. The* ALIEN *laughs mischievously and skips away.*)

SCENE 74. EXTERIOR. NIGHT. BO TREE.

DEVLIN *has had a few pulls at the chillum, and is beginning to feel its effects. His eyes are reddening too. He turns to the sadhu.*

"Wise guy, eh?"

(*The sadhu begins to shimmer a little in his vision.*)

"Tell me somethin'. I wanna jes' sit an' do nothin', jes' like you. Kin I do 't?"

(*The sadhu remains mute and inscrutable. There is a few seconds' pause. Then* DEVLIN *says*)

"Say y' know the rope trick?"

(*No answer.*)

"Y' got a bed o' nails aroun' here somewhere?"

(*Still no answer.*)

"Nah—I bet ya don't. I bet ya sleep on a mattress! Yeah—you're no better 'n Joe Devlin. Maybe not so good. I bet ya can't dig a hole an' strike water—I bet ya can't..."

(DEVLIN *gets up on his feet and walks a few steps. He holds on to a low hanging branch of the Bo tree and looks up at the sky. The full moon has rings around it.* DEVLIN *hums a line of his favourite ballad. Then he addresses the sadhu again.*)

"You see that thing up there? Eh? See that thing? They'll be selling real estate there soon, and the Yanks 're gonna land there, 'n', no kiddin', an' the Reds too. Land on the moon, see? An' that's somethin'. An' it takes a lotta guts to do that, an' a lot o' dough, joo. Y' can't jes' sit 'n' smoke pot 'n' do it, see? Y' gotta be up on yer feet 'n' mov'n'. Y' gotta be on the go. Y' gotta live. Y'r not livin'. Y'r dead. Yeah—y'r dead—as y' got no problems—the dead's got no problems ... no income tax ... no drafts ... no broads ... no busted drainpipes ... Nah! No problems..."

(*The sadhu is staring fixedly at* DEVLIN. *Their eyes meet, and* DEVLIN *falters a little. There is something unnervingly intense about the sadhu's gaze.*)

"Or maybe y' got problems too ... maybe you do ... your yoga an' yer nirvana an' ... an' that temple stickin' outa the pond there!" (DEVLIN *turns and staggers away.*)

SCENE 75. EXTERIOR. NIGHT. BAMBOO FOREST.

In order to go to the drilling site, DEVLIN *has to walk through the bamboo forest. In the forest, in a clearing,* DEVLIN *suddenly comes face to face with the* ALIEN.

DEVLIN *stops dead and stares at the dark childlike form. He leans forward to get a better look. The form shimmers in his vision. The* ALIEN *stands poised on the thin branch of a flowering plant.*

"Hey!" says DEVLIN, "that you, kid?"

(*The* ALIEN *looks on.*)

"Who 'r' you?"

"Wha' ya all keep starin' at me for? Never seen a Yank before? Go on home, beat it."

"Beat it," echoes the ALIEN in a thin, eerie voice.

"Aw, shucks!"

(DEVLIN *turns round and starts walking towards the drilling site. The* ALIEN *hops after him soundlessly.*

DEVLIN *feels he is being followed, stops and turns. The* ALIEN *stops too.*)

"You want bread—*baksheesh*?" DEVLIN fumbles in his pocket and brings out a coin. "Here." He tosses it to the ALIEN and strides away. (*The* ALIEN *picks up the coin, looks at it and laughs happily.*)

Scene 76. Interior. Night. Mohan's bedroom.

MOHAN *and* KALYANI *are in bed, awake. It is obvious that the shy young girl is having difficulty in restraining her newfound emotions.*

"If you would only tell me what's worrying you." There is a slight tremor in her voice.

"I want things to fall in place," says MOHAN, "and they refuse to."

"It's because you let your mind wander too much. You think of the moon and the stars and the zero and ... and don't think of me at all."

(MOHAN *turns to his wife and puts his arms around her.*)

"Why should I think of you when you are right next to me? One worries about a mystery, about something one can't quite understand. You are not a mystery to me!"

"I wish I were—if only to be a little more in your thoughts."

"But you are in my thoughts now, Kalyani…"

"And may I know what those thoughts are?"

"They are thoughts which tell me not to think but to—"

(MOHAN *takes* KALYANI *in a light embrace and kisses her warmly. Then he brings his face very close to hers and keeps looking into her eyes.*)

"What is it you're thinking again?" says KALYANI.

"I'm not thinking. I'm looking. I'm looking at a pond."

"A lotus pond?"

"No, but it's shaped like a lotus petal and it's fringed by dark foliage. There's a vast, round, mysterious temple in the pond which is shaped like a zero. There's a very mischievous deity in it who can take a man's mind off his work and—"

(MOHAN *suddenly stops, frowns.*)

"Stars!" he mutters.

"What stars?"

"Haba said something about stars."

"And now you have to think of Haba," says KALYANI in despair.

"But you don't realize, Kalyani—sometimes a child has more wisdom than an—"

MOHAN suddenly sits up. "Where's that paper?" he says, his eyes shining with excitement.

"What paper?"

"When did we read about that moving light? Yesterday! That means the light was seen two nights ago, and the temple—"

(MOHAN *springs out of bed and rushes out of the room barefooted. Through the mosquito net, we see* KALYANI *sit up with an annoyed pout, her hair falling loose about her equally bare shoulders.*)

SCENE 77. EXTERIOR. NIGHT. LOTUS POND.

MOHAN *comes running and stops by the pond, tense and trembling with excitement. The top of the spaceship glistens in the moonlight and a gentle breeze sways the lotuses.* MOHAN *looks up at the sky, and down again at the spaceship.*

"Haba, where are you? Haba? Where's that little devil gone?" It is the crackly voice of HABA's grandmother.

(MOHAN *turns round and sees the old woman standing outside her shack and looking about helplessly.*)

"Haba! Haba!"

MOHAN runs up to her. "Where's Haba gone?" he asks. "I heard him singing only a little while ago."

"Oh such a pest he is. He was sitting by the pond singing, and I asked him to come to bed, and he said—he said—oh, I don't know what he said."

"Please try to remember what he said. It's very important."

"I'm an old woman. I can't remember. He said—he had a new home, he said ... or something like that. I don't remember—"

(MOHAN *paces about restlessly, unable to decide what he should do. Now* DEVLIN *can be heard, singing his favourite ballad.*)

"If you're travellin' in the north country fair

Where the wind hits heavy on the borderline..."

(MOHAN *dashes off towards the drilling site.*)

Scene 78. Exterior. Night. Drilling site.

MOHAN *rushes up the slope, panting.* DEVLIN *sits slumped in his chair, his legs stretched out, singing to the accompaniment of a guitar.*

"Remember me to one who lives there

She was once a true love of mine…"

"Mr Devlin!"

(*Now* DEVLIN *stops singing and looks up with some displeasure and considerable surprise at* MOHAN.)

MOHAN says, "I'm sorry for coming like this, but there's something I must tell you."

DEVLIN recognizes MOHAN. "You the guy from the newspaper?"

"Yes," says MOHAN, "and I have a strong suspicion that the thing in the pond is not a temple, but a spaceship."

(*It takes a few seconds for this to register on* DEVLIN. *Then he says*)

"American or Russian?"

(*The tone of sarcasm is unmistakable.*

MOHAN *answers in strongly stressed words.*)

"It's not American, and it's not Russian. It's from some other planet. There was a news in the papers yesterday about a moving light seen in the sky from some parts of India. I think that light was a spaceship, and that spaceship has landed in that pond. And I think it has someone in it with super powers, and I think he has caused these miracles to happen."

There is a pause. Then DEVLIN says, "You get paid to think like that?"

"No, but—"

"Then why d'ya think like that? Why don't ya go home to bed and sleep?"

(DEVLIN *takes up his guitar again and starts strumming.*)

"I'm convinced, Mr Devlin. I'm convinced, it's not just a suspicion. It's a certainty. Everything falls into place if you believe it's a spaceship, and from a planet which is far more advanced than ours."

(DEVLIN *stops the guitar, looks* MOHAN *squarely in the face, and says*)

"Okay, so it's a spaceship from Pluto—so what?"

"In that case," says MOHAN, "I think we should do something about it. We should make contact with whoever's in it. We should try to make friends with him. Don't you see, we can learn things from him!"

"Waddya mean *we*? Listen, why doncha go home and write about it? We'll talk to him or her or it when we pump that water out tomorrow…"

"If you go when snowflakes storm,

When rivers freeze…"

MOHAN says, "The water in the pond?"

"And summer ends

…Yeah, so you don't have to swim to church…

Please see she has a coat so warm.

To keep her from the howlin' wind…"

MOHAN says, "You are pumping out the water? It's your idea?"

(DEVLIN stops singing, but keeps strumming the guitar. He says)

"Say, you got a kid livin' around here that goes about in his birthday suit?"

(MOHAN *is in a daze, and* DEVLIN's *question doesn't register on him.*)

"Please see if her hair hangs long…"

"This one's got no hair … and three fingers … must be a leper or something…"

"It rolls and flows all down her breast,

Please see for me if her hair's hanging low…"

MOHAN muses, "But if that thing is not a temple, but a spaceship, and if you start pumping the water out…"

(DEVLIN *loses his temper at last.*)

"Look, lemme ask a simple question—why in the hell's name would a spaceship from Mars or Venus or Jupiter or any other goddam planet or solar system land here? If they're intelligent, why here? They're not Joe Devlin. They got no drillin' job to do for Bajoria!"

"Maybe they came for something you haven't got in the West."

"Yeah—they came for the pot, and it's made 'em a bunch o' sadoos!"

(MOHAN *gets up and turns to go.*

DEVLIN *sings on*)

"I'm wonderin' if she remembers me at all

Many times I've hoped and prayed

In the darkness of my night

In the brightness of my days…"

Fade out.

SCENE 79. EXTERIOR. DAWN OF NEXT DAY. LOTUS POND.

The women of the village, and some of the older men, have already gathered on the shore. They make obeisance, fill their brass pots with the pond water, throw flowers into the pond, etc. BAJORIA's limousine comes bumping up the village path that leads to the pond.

The women around the pond cover their heads with their saris and withdraw into the shade of trees.

The limousine pulls up. A truck carrying the salvage pump lumbers up and pulls up behind it.

Now the whole village turns up at the pond, drawn by the noise of the vehicles. BAJORIA, DEVLIN, *the photographer we have met before with a flash camera, and a police officer get out of the car.* BAJORIA *is dressed in Indian fashion—in a dhoti and a long coat buttoned up to the neck.* DEVLIN *has brought his weapon, a light machine gun, which draws a buzz of comments from the crowd.* BOSE *turns to* PRAMANICK:

"I don't like the look of things at all."

DEVLIN *carries the gun in a very professional manner and there is an extra magazine taped to the one fitted. He walks over towards the pond to have a look.* MOHAN, *unshaven, standing a little away from the crowd, casts a grim look in the direction of the photographer, and then at* BAJORIA. BAJORIA *ignores him and advances towards the crowd with folded palms and a benign smile on his face. The crowd looks stonily back at him. Then he sidles up to the American.* DEVLIN's *inactive muscles get tense.*

Why does he just look on and do nothing?

"What are you waiting for, Joe? Get going—we mustn't give them time to think."

"But I gotta think a little," says DEVLIN his eyes glued on the spaceship, speaking in a barely audible wait-a-minute voice.

"You know, Gug, that looks a damn sight too queer to be a temple—"

"All temples are queer, Joe. There isn't a temple that's unqueer. That is the least queer of all temples in India—"

"And a damn sight too clean to be an old one."

(MOHAN *has moved up. He, too, speaks in a low voice.*)

"That's a spaceship, Mr Devlin."

"What ship? What?" says BAJORIA, turning to MOHAN.

(MOHAN *doesn't answer.*)

Suddenly DEVLIN turns to BAJORIA. "Hold on to this," he says, handing over the gun to him.

Before BAJORIA *can protest, he steps forward and dives into the pond. Another buzz rises from the crowd, and this time there is a clear note of resentment in it. The police officer moves forward, steeling himself for an emergency.*

MOHAN *watches tensely.* KALYANI *moves forward to stand beside him, holding on to his arm.*

SCENE 80. EXTERIOR. DAY. LOTUS POND. UNDERWATER.

DEVLIN *makes his way through the lotuses and reaches the capsule. He clambers up the curved side, finds the crystalline viewport and is trying to look inside, when the capsule begins to throb.*

DEVLIN *dives back into the water and swims rapidly to the shore.*

SCENE 81. EXTERIOR. DAY. LOTUS POND.

He climbs up the slope, stands panting and waves his hand at the capsule.

"You got the first live temple in history out there."

(*The red glow of the just risen sun now pervades the lotus pond. A strange silence sweeps over the crowd. The birds too fall silent in the dawn.*

Now it is DEVLIN *who breaks the spell.*)

"Explosives!" he yells. "Singh! Get the explosives!"

(SINGH *and most of the other workers are in the crowds and they make a dash towards the drilling site.*

DEVLIN *snatches the gun away from* BAJORIA'*s hand and fairly screams into his ears.*)

"Drive to the nearest phone booth—call the US Embassy—call the Army Headquarters—tell them to send help—it's an emergency—there's a spaceship here and it's a source of danger ... GO!"

BAJORIA, "Danger! Danger..."

(BAJORIA *bundles himself into the car, followed by his entourage. The villagers now run helter-skelter in panic, leaving the pond almost deserted with the exception of* DEVLIN, MOHAN *and his wife,* BAJORIA *and his party, and the dredging personnel.*

MOHAN, *white as a sheet, turns to* KALYANI *and says*)

"For heaven's sake, leave this place."

"I'm not going," says KALYANI firmly, "as long as you're here."

(DEVLIN *has run up to the truck and hauls out a stout wire rope with the help of some workers.*

BAJORIA'*s car swerves round, but the chauffeur has lost his nerve and runs the car into a tree.*

A light, the same light that we saw shining in the first scene—now begins to pulsate through the walls of the capsule and a strange musical hum begins. And over the hum begins the song. This is HABA'*s song sung in a weird, metallic, unearthly voice. The capsule begins to rise slowly revealing for the first time the shape of the lower half that was below the surface of the water.*

DEVLIN *watches tensely. Suddenly the viewport of the capsule—now seen clearly—flashes red as it catches the rising sun.)*

DEVLIN shouts, "Get down everyone, dive under cover."

(*Rolling into cover, he aims his gun at the window and fires a burst of shots at it. Inside the spaceship, the* ALIEN *sits as before, completely confused about what is happening around the pond. The song brings the crowd trickling back to the pond and everyone stares speechlessly at the capsule which is now bathed in the light of the sun. Against the red glow it is still emitting its own strange light which throbs to the rhythm of the song.*

HABA*'s grandma has come out of her shack.)*

"Haba!" she cries out. "Where are you? Where have you been all this time?"

Cut to

SCENE 80. INTERIOR. DAY. CABIN OF SPACESHIP.

The ALIEN *sits crosslegged, in the classical manner of the Buddha, a red disc of sunlight on his face and around his head, singing the simple song about flowers and rivers and paddy fields that* HABA *has taught him.*

Around the ALIEN*—in this gravity-less cabin of the spaceship—floats* HABA, *in a state of blissful slumber, and the various specimens of earthly flora and fauna he has helped to collect for his "friend"—a frog, a firefly, a snake, a fish, a lotus, a squirrel and a bulbul bird—all in a state of suspended animation.*

The ALIEN *now stops singing and stretches his hand towards an invisible control.*

SCENE 81. EXTERIOR. DAY. LOTUS POND.

There is a sudden hissing sound, and the capsule is enveloped in a greenish vapour.

The hum spirals to a long, high pitch and the spaceship vanishes. The vapour spreads over the pond. The lotuses all droop and wither. The paddy, the fruits, and the flowers all go back to their original state.

"Jezzus!" says DEVLIN, the first to find speech. He slumps down flat on the grass still dripping from his swim. He hangs his head down, shakes it several times, then he looks up at MOHAN, grins and says, "Well, buddy, guess you can go write that story now!"

MOHAN, still in a sort of trance, says, "As soon as I've found the words."

(KALYANI *as white as a sheet but happy and relaxed rests her tired head on her husband's shoulder.*

Now DEVLIN *turns to* BAJORIA. *He is sitting on the grass, legs stretched out, a dazed look in his eyes.)*

Above: Ray exploring the rural setting for the film; *Below:* Subrata Mitra taking test shots

"You want the water pumped out, Gug?"

(BAJORIA *has a glassy look in his eyes, and his lips are curled up in an idiot-smile. He starts clapping his hands robot-like and begins to hum his favourite bhajan.*)

"*Papa papa pum pa papa…*"

(*The clapping now extends to the crowd but this is not to keep time for* BAJORIA's *singing, but to applaud* DEVLIN. DEVLIN *turns to the crowd. All eyes are turned on him. The cheering is infectious, and spreads. Someone says in Bengali*)

"Great show, Mr America!"

(*This is immediately echoed by other sections of the crowd.*)

BOSE says, "Well, there are good Americans and bad Americans. This one's a good one."

(*A puzzled* DEVLIN *turns to* MOHAN *for enlightenment.*)

"What the hell's going on?"

"They're cheering you," says MOHAN.

"But why?"

"They think you've saved them."

"Saved them? I saved them?"

"… from the Alien's magic, Mr Devlin. They weren't too happy about the miracles."

"Jesus Christ!" says DEVLIN, getting up on his feet. "Do I take a bow?" Then he turns to BAJORIA. "You see what you've got me into, Gug? They think I'm a comicbook Superman."

(*The cheering is now deafening.*

DEVLIN *can only shake his head, dazed by what to him is a totally unexpected turn of events.*)

"Oh, no!" he mutters. "No, no, no!"

(*Then he starts walking past the pond, away from the crowd, his body shaken by a wild, uncontrollable laughter at the monumental absurdity of his predicament.*

The gun in his hand is the only absurdity he can do something about.

He flings it into the pond.

It descends on a hunch of broad lotus leaves, causing a startled frog to leap clear.

Then it slithers off the leaves and sinks into the pond, sending up bubbles.)

THE ALIEN SCRIPT FOR COLUMBIA (EXCERPTS)*

THE ALIEN

A Treatment

By

Satyajit Ray

*The corrections in the scripts are made by Ray himself

THE ALIEN

A Treatment

By

Satyajit Ray

Property of Mike J. Wilson and
Satyajit Ray
Indus International Productions
at the office of
Louis C. Blau
9777 Wilshire Boulevard
Beverly Hills, California

-1-

Night. A lotus pond in the village of

Mangalpur in West Bengal. The camera holds

on a part of the surface of the pond with *lit by a br?t moonlight,*

lotus leaves and limp lotus stalks, A

point of light appears as a reflection in

the water, grows bigger and bigger until the

pond itself is lit up. The chorus of frógs,

crickets and jackals grows in volume, and is

joined by a humming sound. In a blaze of light

something descends on the pond, shattering

its placidity. A cascade of water descends on

the lotus leaves, and the camera tilts up and

zooms back to a full shot of the pond.

A domelike object is seen sinking into the water.

The pulsating light that emanates from it dims

into total darkness as the object slowly dis-

appears below the surface.

As the surface calms down, in the deadly silence

that now pervades, all the limp lotus stalks

straighten up and open their petals at the

same time.

-2-

TITLES begin over this shot.

Sc 2. Lotus pond, Exterior, Day

With the last titles, moonlight changes into the light of morning.

A song sung casually in a boyish voice is heard - a simple touching folk ballad about the beauty of flowers and birdsong and fields of grass and paddy.

The camera pans to show a bamboo forest by the pond, and in that forest a little boy is collecting twigs, and singing. The boy is dressed in rags, and is obviously very poor. In the background, a bent old woman is seen sweeping out dry bamboo leaves from around a shack made of twigs and dry coconut leaves.

Sc 3. Bamboo Grove, Ext, Day

The boy HABA picks up a twig, straightens up, and catches sight of the lotuses in the pond. His singing stops and his mouth falls open. Then he turns to the old woman and shouts: 'Grandma, come and see the lotuses!'

-53-

Haba's grandma has come out of her shack.
'Haba!' she cries out. 'Where are you? Where
have you been all this time?'

CUT TO

INSIDE THE CAPSULE.

The Alien sits crosslegged, in the classical

manner of the Buddha, a red disc of sunlight

on his face and around his head, singing the

simple song about flowers and rivers and paddy

fields that Haba has taught him.

　　Around the Alien - in this gravity-less

cabin of the spaceship - float Haba, in a

state of blissful slumber, and the various

specimens of earthly flora and fauna he has

helped to collect for his 'friend' - a frog,

a firefly, a snake, a fish, a lotus, a squirrel

and a bulbul bird - all in a state of suspended

animation.

The Alien now stretches his hand toward an

invisible control.

THE LOTUS POND.

There is a sudden hissing sound, and the capsule

is enveloped in a greenish vapour. A high-

-55-

A puzzled Devlin turns to Mohan for enlightenment.

'What the hell's going on?'

'They think you did it,' says Mohan.

'I did it?' Utter disbelief in Devlin's
voice.

Mohan nods.

'You mean - you mean - they think it's
something I rigged up for them? A kinda SHOW?'

Mohan nods again.

'Jesus Christ!' says Devlin, getting up
on his feet. 'Do I take a Bow?'

The cheering is now deafening.

Devlin can only shake his head, dazed by the
totally unexpected turn of events. 'Unbelievable'
he mutters - 'Unbelievable'.

Then he starts walking, past the pond, away
from the crowd, his body shaken by a wild,
uncontrollable laughter at the monumental
absurdity of his predicament.

The gun in his hand is the only absurdity
he can do something about.

He flings it into the pond.

The gun descends on a bunch of broad lotus
leaves causing a startled frog to leap clear.

Then it slithers off the leaves and sinks into
the pond.

THE END.

THE ALIEN SCRIPT NOTEBOOK (EXCERPTS)

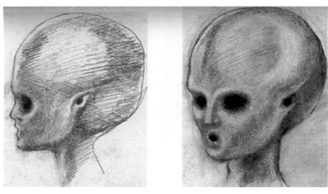

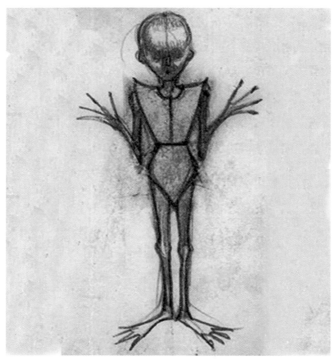

Sketches of the Alien by Ray

Cover page of the draft treatment, 24 February 1967.
Ray had three names in mind: *Avatar*, *Mangal-kabya* (Martian tales) and *The Alien*

(3)

The AVATAR

Place: Mangalpur, a village in West Bengal

Time: ~~Midnight in the~~ early hours of ~~morning on a~~ month of August with the moon at full.

PRE-CREDITS SEQUENCE

We see the surface of a fairly large pond which is largely covered with lotus leaves. It is full moon tonight, and in the reflection in the pond one can see the silhouette you cannot the silhouetted against the sky.

A point of light appears in the reflection & grows bigger & bigger until the lotus leaves are lit up.

The chorus of frogs & crickets & jackals grows in volume is joined by a ~~tinkle of~~ unpleasant humming noise surface stolen by the surface of a tree crescendo until the water surface ~~agitated~~ by something striking it. The disc of light almost fills the frame. Then we hear a ~~status~~ swish as ... in the reflection ... a coconut tree in the reflection arching down ... the ~~impact of the~~ ... at an it is hit by the disc, while ... next proceeds to land on the water, shattering its placidity. A cascade of water drenches the lotus leaves, & the camera at

First page of the draft treatment

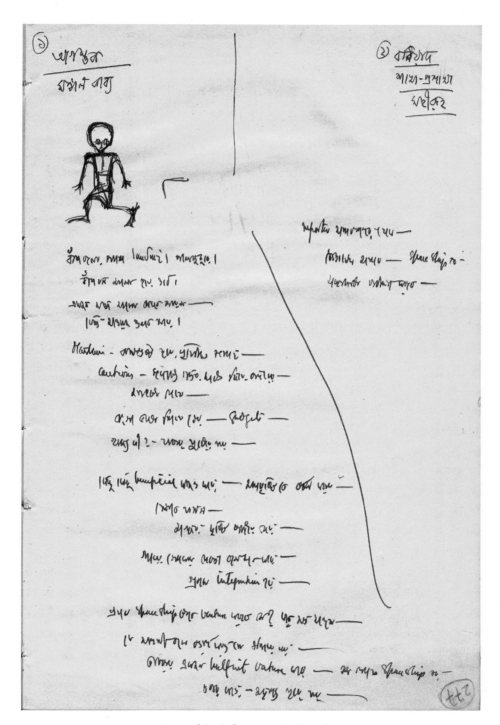

A page of the draft treatment in Bengali

THE ALIEN: AN INTERVIEW WITH SATYAJIT RAY

ASCHORJO MAGAZINE, 1967

Satyajit Ray had plans to make *The Alien* a bilingual project. The Bengali film was to be named *Avatar*. Ray gave an interview on *The Alien* to *ASCHORJO*, a Bengali sci-fi magazine, in two parts in 1967. The first part came out in May and the second in September. ADRISH BARDHAN, editor of the magazine, conducted the interview.

PART I

ADRISH BARDHAN: For which character in the film did you choose Peter Sellers? Which country is Sellers from?

SATYAJIT RAY: I chose Peter Sellers for a Marwari character in my film. He is an Englishman who stayed in Calcutta for a full year during the War (World War II).

ADRISH: Will he speak Bengali in your film?

SATYAJIT: Sellers won't have to speak Bengali in my film. He will speak in English to an American. However, he has a strong desire to speak Bengali. He made me an earnest request (to allow him to speak English). I gave him my word that I would arrange an opportunity for him to speak Bengali.

ADRISH: Will Marlon Brando play the American?

SATYAJIT: It is a remote possibility because he is not suitable for the story of my film. Besides, I was told in London that Brando is temperamental. He is not an easy actor to work with.

ADRISH: But Brando is keen on working with you.

SATYAJIT: That's true. I got an opportunity to meet him when he suddenly came to Calcutta. He loves my films, so much so that he seeks out each of my films and sees it.

ADRISH: Don't you think that Brando has a strong appeal to lay viewers?

SATYAJIT: That's right indeed. But I have Steve McQueen in mind. He is an extraordinary actor. He has acquired a reputation in the last four or five years. That apart, he is admirably fit for my character. Those who have seen *The Great Escape* will never forget him. He reminds one of the Humphrey Bogart of *Casablanca*.

ADRISH: Steve McQueen is a busy actor. What will you do if he does not have time?

SATYAJIT: In that case, I'd like to take Paul Newman on.

ADRISH: Do you have plans to go to Hollywood?

SATYAJIT: Yes, I shall go in the month of May.

ADRISH: Have you decided on the title of your film?

SATYAJIT: The name of the English film is *The Alien*. The Bengali edition of the film will probably be named *Avatar*.

ADRISH: How is Arthur C. Clarke associated with you in this project?

SATYAJIT: In all probability, he will not be associated with this project because the story has already been written without his contribution. I am free in this respect, but he will work with me when the story comes out in the form of a novel.

ADRISH: But *Avatar* is being written in Bengali...

SATYAJIT: Yes. But, based on this story, Arthur C. Clarke will write a novel which will be distributed around the world from London. Clarke and I will be credited as co-authors.

ADRISH: Then this is going to be the first 70mm movie made in India and the first Indian sci-fi film at that.

SATYAJIT: Yes. The cameraman, the make-up man and the spaceship will come from abroad.

ADRISH: That means a lot of money.

SATYAJIT: My partner Mike Wilson is financing the film. He has made four to five films in Ceylon, making 500 per cent profits from each of his films. He has told me not to worry about money which will come from America. I feel I will be happy working with them. I haven't got such a set-up ever (to make a film) before.

ADRISH: When will you start working on the film?

SATYAJIT: Mike wants the work to begin in the month of September. In that case, it will be possible to release the film sometime next year (1968). I wanted to begin the sci-fi film after finishing *Asani Sanket* (*The Distant Thunder*) and *Goopy Gyne Bagha Byne*

(*The Adventures of Goopy and Bagha*) because the way I make films will have changed after I had made this film. Mike Wilson too thinks as much. But ultimately it was decided that work on the film would begin in January next year. Otherwise we may face some problems. *Asani Sanket* will have been shot by that time.

ADRISH: What about *Goopy Gyne Bagha Byne*?

SATYAJIT: I'll shoot it in October next year.

ADRISH: Is Mike Wilson an American?

SATYAJIT: He was born in England. He joined the Merchant Navy and visited many countries. He stayed in Canada for a long time.

PART II

This part of the interview was conducted after Satyajit Ray had returned from the US.

ADRISH: Have you finalized all the formalities for making the sci-fi film?

SATYAJIT: More or less. But I have to go to America once more along with the technicians.

ADRISH: When will you start shooting the film?

SATYAJIT: Work will begin in October next year. We need three to four months for preparations before we start working.

ADRISH: Have you roped in Steve McQueen?

SATYAJIT: No. He is not available for the next two years. So, I have decided to take a rising actor. He has begun to build up a reputation in Hollywood. I will get the news (of whether I will get him for my film) in seven days. It will be a good break for him.

ADRISH: Who are the technicians who will work on this film?

SATYAJIT: I'll have to take my cameraman Subrata Mitra and art director Bansi Chandragupta along to Hollywood before the shooting begins.

ADRISH: Will you shoot the film with a 70mm camera?

SATYAJIT: No, the film will be shot with a small 35mm camera. There are two advantages. First, we won't have the trouble of moving a big camera from one place to another. Secondly, there are not many theatres for screening 70mm films in the world. We'll shoot the film in 35mm from which we can easily get 70mm prints. That's what everybody does.

ADRISH: Is there a possibility that you will engage the services of a foreign cameraman?

SATYAJIT: I have received such an offer. Haskell Wexler, a top cameraman in Hollywood, wrote to me saying that he wanted to work for my film, and that he won't take any money for his services.

ADRISH: Who produces your film?

SATYAJIT: Columbia Pictures. They are also the world distributors for my film. Mike Wilson and I have launched a company for making the film. This is the first time that such an arrangement has been made in Asia (for making a film).

Translated from the Bengali by **ARUP K. DE**

SATYAJIT RAY AND THE ALIEN

AMITA MALIK

SIGHT AND SOUND, WINTER 1967

B oth as a film-maker and a person, Satyajit Ray seems so far removed from science fiction that Indians were as intrigued as rest of the world when news leaked out that Ray was going to shoot a science fiction film in Calcutta with Peter Sellers playing an Indian. But, as with all his films, Ray has planned every step with calm deliberation and apparent enjoyment. To my questions—Why Peter Sellers? Will science fiction be box-office in India? Could he please tell me a little about the plot?—Ray gave answers as lucid as they are logical. But I shall respect his wish not to give away too much of the plot, since he does not start shooting for a year. I shall quote his own words on *The Alien*:

1) "I have three main reasons for casting Peter Sellers, a) My great admiration for him: it's good to work with a real virtuoso once in a while. b) I thought it would be fun to see him playing an Indian in an Indian film, and I thought the idea would intrigue Sellers too (I was right). c) *The Alien* needs top technical quality, with special effects in colour, etc. Which meant processing abroad—which meant bigger cost—which called for a wider market to bring back that cost—which meant British/American distribution to exploit that market—which called for a big name in the cast to interest the distribution company—which meant Sellers."

2) "*The Alien* is not 100 per cent science fiction because the emphasis is really more on the human aspect, on human reactions to an SF situation, which is an SF situation only towards the end. Before that, it is more a religious-superstitious situation. With more than half of the dialogue in English, *The Alien* is not aimed at the wider Indian

market. I expect it will play on the circuit that foreign (American/British) films play, with the Bengali bits subtitled in English (same procedure for G.B. and U.S.A.)."

3) The plot centres on "an unidentified spaceship descending silently and unnoticed by anyone in a lotus pond on the outskirts of a small Bengali village. The village has its contingent of peasants, middle-class inhabitants, a school, post-office, etc." A young couple from Calcutta is also on a visit, the husband being a journalist who is doing an on-the-spot study for a series of articles on the *Changing Face of the Village*. Other characters are an American engineer, and the Marwari industrialist (Peter Sellers), who has engaged him to sink a well. "The alien is supremely intelligent, endowed with super-powers, but puckish in its ways," says Ray. "When he leaves, the human beings, rich and poor, white and brown, primitive and sophisticated, are all in an identical state of stupefied helplessness."

Satyajit Ray has written his own screenplay for *The Alien*; and he will also be writing the music.

ORDEALS OF THE ALIEN

SATYAJIT RAY
THE *STATESMAN*, CALCUTTA, 4 & 5 OCTOBER 1980

"Sellers is in Paris," said Mike Wilson, putting down the telephone. "They"ll get in touch with him and find out if he's interested."

"They" were Peter Sellers's agents in London, whom Mike had called up from my flat in Calcutta's Lake Temple Road within minutes of learning that I was thinking of approaching the British actor to play the part of an Indian businessman in my projected science-fiction film, *The Alien*. While by no means a blockbuster in the Hollywood sense, the special effects in the film alone called for a budget which was high by Indian standards. If the money was to come from Hollywood, a big name or two in the cast would help, and Sellers was certainly in that category. Moreover, he was a fine, rangey actor, and he had already played an Indian in a Hollywood film, *The Millionairess*. If, as I suspected, he knew only one kind of Indian accent—a vaguely South Indian one—I was sure that if he agreed to play in *The Alien*, he wouldn't mind making an effort to add a new and authentic one to his repertoire. The two LPs of his that I possessed held proof that he could do things with his voice and tongue which bordered on the miraculous.

PROMISING

Mike Wilson had come with credentials from the noted astronomer and science fiction writer Arthur C. Clarke. I had met Clarke in London the year before and described to him the germ of an idea I had for a sci-fi film. Clarke had found it promising. Back home in Colombo, he had talked about it to his friend Mike Wilson. Wilson too had settled in Colombo, marrying a Sinhalese Christian of striking good looks. He had also elbowed his way into the film business; written, produced and directed *James Banda*, blithely transplanting the Fleming secret service agent in Sri Lanka and rounded up virtually the entire European community of Colombo to play sinister bit roles in the film. Above all, Mike was a highly skilled professional skin diver with the legendary distinction of having stumbled upon a seventeenth-century Mughal galleon off the coast of Sri Lanka, and retrieved from the wreck a chestful of silver coins. When a man like that writes and tells you that he is ready to give his right arm to set up a co-production deal with you, you are inclined to take his word on trust.

But I had to write and tell Mr Wilson that there was nothing on paper yet beyond a few jottings. Undaunted, he flew down to Calcutta, checked into a Sudder Street hotel and announced that he would stick around until I produced a treatment. I thought it prudent to tell him that writing being an intensely private pursuit with me, I discouraged company while working on a script. Mike ignored my stricture. "I shall sit by and make coffee for you when you need it, Maestro."

Mike didn't make coffee, but sit by me he did and, being a friend of Arthur C. Clarke, kept tossing off ideas which slid off the pages of my script. By the end of a fortnight, I had a treatment.

Meanwhile, word had come that Sellers was interested.

Mike and I turned up in Paris in the April of 1967 and met Sellers in his hotel. "New Zealand?" asked Sellers as soon as Mike opened his mouth. Mike nodded, grinning. I was duly impressed. We sat and talked about sundry matters over lunch in the vast hotel dining room. Sellers knew no French but spoke "Franglaise" which had the waiters in stitches. Half a dozen of them had thronged round our table, some with autograph albums. Inspector Clouseau had gone over big in Paris. "Do you know my work at all?" I found an occasion to inquire, not with some trepidation. "No," said Sellers. "But Jonathan Miller swears by you, and his word is good enough for me." But it wasn't good enough for me. I asked Mike if he could somehow set up a screening of one of my films for Sellers while in Paris. Mike dialled London from Sellers's suite and a print of *Charulata* arrived from the London distributors the next morning. We screened it in a mini viewing theatre the same day. As the film ended and the lights came up a red-eyed Sellers turned to me and said : "Why do you need me? I'm not better than your actors, you know!" Of course, Sellers knew why we needed him. He was just being modest. At any rate he heard the story, said he liked the part, and asked Mike to keep in touch with his agents. Soon after this, Mike and I parted. He had to see about the fate of *James Banda* in Sri Lanka while pursuing *The Alien* and I to sit at home and await word from him.

Ray in Paris. Photograph by Mike Wilson

Ray in Los Angeles. Photograph by Mike Wilson

JOYOUS

The next communication from Mike, a month later, was from Hollywood. It was a joyous carillon of a cable: Columbia will back *The Alien*; I was to be given free hand; both Brando and Steve McQueen were keen to play the American engineer; Saul Bass will mastermind the special effects etc., etc. Sellers was in Hollywood too, playing an Indian in a comedy, and anxious to have a second session with me.

With the hum of the machinery in my ears, I arrived in Hollywood on 1 June. Mike drove me into town from the airport in a hired Lincoln convertible and I found myself checking into the Chateau Marmont, an elegant, self-contained two-storied cottage with all mod cons, one of several which dotted the lawns of the hotel Marmont where, as I learned later, Maurice Chevalier had once maintained a permanent suite. "Don't worry, Maestro," said Mike, reading the signs of solicitude which I must have betrayed. "Columbia has made an advance against expenses. You can't afford anything but the best, you know, you made the *Apu Trilogy!*"

The first meeting with Sellers was at Ravi Shankar's place. The Indian part in the new comedy called for his going through the motions of playing the sitar and Sellers was anxious to get the fingering right. Ravi had promised to play after dinner.

With simple Bengali dishes backed by superb North Indian contributions from Ravi Shankar's gifted accompanist, Alla Rakha, the dinner was an unqualified success.

Ravi Shankar, Wilson and Alla Rakha. Photograph by Satyajit Ray

During the splendid recital that followed, Sellers sat cross-legged on the carpet, intently watchful, and simulated learned response by judicious interjections of wah-wahs. On the way back, I asked him what kind of an Indian he was playing in the new film. "It's a film about a chap who lands up in Hollywood to play a bit part in a North-West Frontier movie, and gets invited to a big Hollywood party by mistake. The film is called *The Party*."

"What's the Indian called?" I knew Sellers was partial to the name Bannerji.

"Bakshi," said Sellers and then made a noise like a snorting rhino.

"What's that?"

"First name," said Sellers, "H-R-U-N-D-I, Hrundi V. Bakshi. You must come and watch the shooting. Blake's a genius at improvising comic business. The other day we shot a hilarious scene where the chap gets swathed in a roll of toilet paper."

I tried to sound casual as I mentioned that, unlike the starring roles he's been playing of late, in *The Alien* he would have to share the honours with three others: the Bengali journalist hero, the American engineer and the wordless, elfin creature from outer space.

HILARIOUS

Sellers said that he didn't mind at all. "And I'll tell you one thing: I had an Indian astrologer tell me in London that I was going to work with an Indian director. So that is as much an act of volition as a decree of fate." On the strength of the one *Pink Panther* film I had seen, Blake Edwards hadn't struck me as a director of much comic talent. Sellers himself had appeard much less funny as Inspector Clouseau than, for instance, in the hilarious first episode of the seven-part De Sica film, *Seven Times, Woman*. I mentioned how good I thought he was in this film.

"Did you?"

Sellers sounded dubious. Then he shook his head, dismissing my judgment—"That De Sica," he grumbled, "insists on acting out everything. And then wants you to copy him. I was most unhappy."

Peter Sellers shooting for *The Party*. Photograph by Satyajit Ray

Peter Sellers and Britt Eklund. Photograph by Satyajit Ray

Sellers was obviously happy working under Blake Edwards. The day we went, they were shooting the key scene—the scene of the party. Between takes, Sellers kept snuggling to his newly married second wife, the Swedish Britt Eklund. Sellers had suffered a heart attack some months ago and Eklund saw to it that he didn't overstrain himself. A dozen or so Hollywood movie types sat around a table and ate. They included an Amazonian blonde and a cowboy with a gun in a holster. Sellers, the odd man out, sat next to the blonde on a stool so low that his chin nuzzled the table cloth. I stood

"I stood close enough ... to catch Hrundi eyeing the blonde's cleavage..."

close enough during the take to catch Hrundi eyeing the blonde's cleavage while he ad-libbed, "My friend Bannerrrji whom I met in Worrrli last February..." He also daubed butter on his thumb instead of the toast he held in his hand an inch away.

I know that most comedians are funny on the screen because they are given funny things to do and say by their directors, writers and gagmen. Even Groucho never spoke his own lines. But Groucho had the skill to put over his lines with style; and the best of his writers, such as Perelman knew precisely what would bring out the best in him. This is a convention of film comedy which one accepts and it doesn't belittle the achievements of the truly gifted comedian. His skill, like a musician's, is interpretative and one judges him on that level. But it is surely not right when a comedian with the calibre of Sellers cheerfully submits to the whims of a director who can think only in terms of belly-laughs, many of which were clearly not going to come off on the screen. Did Sellers not care enough? Or did he lack judgment? He was certainly superb in all the three parts he played in Kubrick's *Dr Strangelove* a couple of years ago.

Peter Sellers photographed by Satyajit Ray

Outwardly, at least, Sellers's enthusiasm for *The Alien* didn't wane during my stay in Hollywood, although the project didn't get off the ground. Columbia were truly keen, but why—I was asked by the young executive who was looking after this particular "property"—did I need Mike Wilson? Who was he? How did I come to team up with him? I had been asking myself the same questions. I had found, upon arriving in Hollywood, mimeographed copies of my script piled up on a table in the room marked "Office" in the cottage where he stayed. They bore the surprising legend: "Copyright: Mike Wilson & Satyajit Ray". I had questioned Mike and he had explained it was to make doubly sure that my interests were protected. "Two heads are better than one, Maestro." Beyond suggesting that I use the term "broad" instead of "chick" in the American's dialogue, Mike had made no contribution to the screenplay that I could think of.

THE PARTY

Since no one walks in Los Angeles (you can be held up for vagrancy, if you do), there was plenty of time for me to sit alone in the cottage and wonder where all this bizarrerie was leading to. A party at Jennifer Jones's in the vast mansion once occupied by Greta Garbo and John Gilbert only heightened the feeling of having strayed into a Carrollian Wonderland. One met stars and actors of the 1940s—Olivia de Havilland, Rita Hayworth, William Wyler, King Vidor—that one scarcely believed existed in the flesh. And in the midst of all this, Mike vanished from view, and then suddenly materialized through a door on the far side of the party room, to drag me off whispering, "Come and see Johns in the john, Maestro,"—and sure enough, I found no less than six Augustus John drawings on the walls of one of the most spacious and elegant bathrooms I've ever seen.

I left Hollywood firmly convinced that *The Alien* was doomed. In fact, the snuffing out took longer than I expected. Shortly after my return to Calcutta, I got a letter from Sellers. It was in verse. Sellers had asked me in Hollywood if I knew the poetry of William McGonagall. I had to confess I didn't. "What? You don't know the greatest Bad Verse writer of all time?" Sellers, it seemed, had regaled his audience with recitals of McGonagall in his Goon Show days. Scottish by birth, this "Poet and Tragedian"—as he styled himself—flourished in the latter part of nineteenth century, wrote narrative poetry, had found a publisher, and built up a following. Sellers went to the length of procuring two of his books for me in Hollywood and ticking the verses he liked best. A single quotation will suffice to give non-afficionados an idea of the kind of verse McGonagall wrote. The following concludes "The Tay Bridge Disaster":

Oh! Ill fated Bridge of the Silv'ry Tay
I must now conclude my lay
By telling the world fearlessly without the least dismay
That your central girders wouldn't have given way
At least many sensible men do say
Had they been supported on each side by buttresses
At least many sensible men confesses
For the stronger we our houses do build
The less chance we have of being killed.

Sellers had just seen *Pather Panchali*. He wrote:

In the year of 1967 and in the month of December
An auspicious month coming as it does at the end of the year
And not the slightest alike to November
Is a month I will long remember.
I received one day
From Satyajit Ray
Information I required without delay
So that I could say to my friends the evening of that day

The film you are about to see
Is the film of a Trilogy
And is called Pather Panchali
In which there is a scene of two children in a field of barley
Watching a train go by
Under an azure sky
So beautiful you want to die.
etc.

Soon after this, *The Alien* took me on another trip, this time to London. The project had been transferred from Columbia USA to Columbia UK, whatever that meant, and the bosses in London were anxious to have a talk with me. Mike preceded me by a week and booked me into a suite at Hilton's. What was left of the Columbia advance apparently still permitted such luxury. Mike was his usual ebullient self, called me Maestro, and touched my feet when high on pot. I had discovered his addiction early on in Calcutta, and I must say it had come as a surprise. Far from being the long-haired, unkempt type, Mike was among the trimmest and sprucest men I have known. But being a square in appearance didn't prevent him from being Pied Piper to the Flower People on Sunset Strip in Hollywood, who came droopily trailing behind him every evening into the living room of the Chateau Marmont to turn the place into a Hippie Haunt.

SON-ET-LUMIERE

In London, at the Hilton, I usually kept to my room, but had to go and see Mike one evening in his suite two floors below mine. The scene that met my eyes through the pall of smoke could have been a set piece out of Petronius. The carpet was strewn with bodies, male and female, and Subbulakshmi sang above the whirr of a movie projector and the Bengali dialogue of what turned out to be a 16mm print of my own film *Devi*, flickering fitfully on a bare wall on one side of the room, a son et lumiere to end all son et lumieres.

But I was more concerned about Mike sober than Mike high, because it was when he had his wits about him that he revealed some alarming new facets. He had never bugged phone calls before, but he did this time, every call which had to do with our project. And he had started carrying a small cassette recorder in his briefcase which he turned on surreptitiously to record every scrap of conversation in the offices of Columbia. "They're a nasty lot here," he said to me as I questioned the ethics of the operation. "I'd

Mike Wilson in his office. Photograph by Satyajit Ray

Mike Wilson in Paris. Photograph by Satyajit Ray

like to see them go back on their word now." I had only one meeting with Columbia where Mike was not present. "Have you got the 10,000 dollar advance which Mr Wilson received on your behalf for your screenplay?" they asked me. I said I wasn't even aware such an advance had been made. By now I had begun to feel like a full-fledged Kafka hero. Mike was supposed to be associate producer, but there was as yet no agreement between us. He was anxious to make good the lacuna. On my way to the airport—Mike had commissioned a Rolls with a built-in cocktail cabinet for the journey—a sheaf of papers was slapped down on my knee—"if you would just sign here, Maestro."

I said: "I'm sorry. I can't even read what I'm supposed to sign."

Mike zipped out a pocket torch and flashed it on the top page of the bunch.

"It's just to say you and I are partners."

"I can't sign anything in a car, Mike," I said. "Not even in a Rolls-Royce. Send the papers over to me in Calcutta."

"KEEP SEETHA"

I waited, but the papers didn't come. A production man from Columbia UK came down to Calcutta a few months later. He said Columbia would back the film if Mike could be persuaded to pull out. "Only you can do it, Mr Ray," said Nick Macdonald. "Write to him. Who knows, he may yet be persuaded to see reason." I wrote to Mike asking him to forgo his copyright on the screenplay so I could proceed on my own. Mike sent a sizzling reply calling me a thief and a slanderer. And no question of parting with the rights naturally. Peter wrote next. This time in prose. "I should tell you straightaway," he said, "that though the part may appear more or less complete to you it does not seem so to me and I don't see how I could contemplate playing it as it is." I had told Peter that the screenplay was a first draft and would be fleshed out—though not to any great extent. All he had to do at this stage was to agree in principle—which he did. I wrote back:

> *Dear Peter, if you had wanted a bigger part,*
> *Why, you should have told me right at the start,*
> *By disclosing it at this juncture*
> *You have surely punctured*
> *The Alien—balloon*
> *Which I daresay will now be grounded soon*
> *Causing a great deal of dismay*
> *To Satyajit Ray.*

There was no answer from Peter. I had in the meantime seen *The Party*, and noted the nod (or was it a dig?) at *Pather Panchali* at the end of the film. "I'm sorry," says Bakshi to the girl who has taken a fancy to him and has asked him into her flat. "I'm sorry, but I must go back to my monkey." "Monkey!" "Yes. My pet monkey, Apu." For over a year there was no communication from anybody on *The Alien* and the project for me receded into the realms of the unattainable. Then, unexpectedly, came a brief note from Arthur C. Clarke. Mike had shaved his head and gone off to the jungles of South India to meditate.

This was followed by a letter from the shaven-headed monk himself. He was relinquishing his rights to the screenplay, although obviously too close to sainthood to spell it out in mundane terms. This is the way he chose to put it.

Dear Ravana:
You may keep Seetha. She's yours. Keep her, and make her and the world happy.

CORRESPONDENCES AND NEWS REPORTS

Steve McQueen photographed by Satyajit Ray

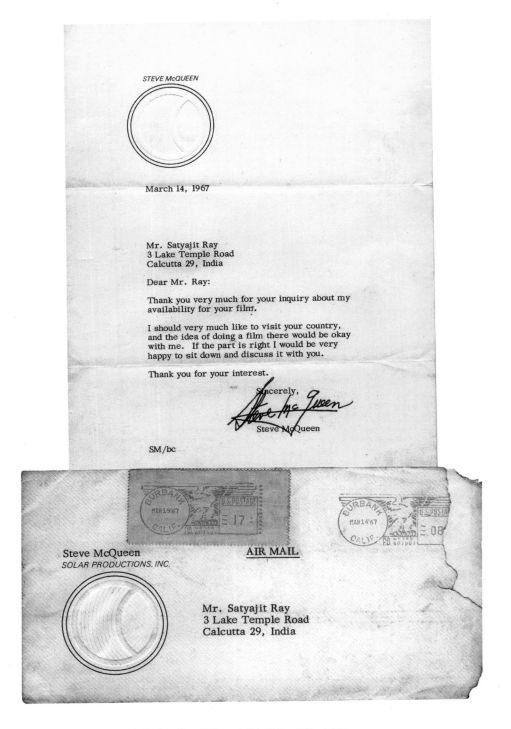

STEVE McQUEEN

March 14, 1967

Mr. Satyajit Ray
3 Lake Temple Road
Calcutta 29, India

Dear Mr. Ray:

Thank you very much for your inquiry about my
availability for your film.

I should very much like to visit your country,
and the idea of doing a film there would be okay
with me.   If the part is right I would be very
happy to sit down and discuss it with you.

Thank you for your interest.

Sincerely,

Steve McQueen

SM/bc

Steve McQueen
SOLAR PRODUCTIONS. INC.

AIR MAIL

Mr. Satyajit Ray
3 Lake Temple Road
Calcutta 29, India

Letter from Steve McQueen to Satyajit Ray, 14 March 1967

Stanley Kubrick at Elstree Studios photographed by Satyajit Ray

STANLEY KUBRICK

9th May, 1967.

Mr. Satyajit Ray,
3 Lake Temple Road,
Calcutta 29,
India.

Dear Satyajit,

Thank you very much for your note. I hope that everything goes well with Mike in Hollywood. As you know, he is working with my attorney, Louis Blau, who, as well as being one of the most knowledgeable and experienced film lawyers, is also a great admirer of your films. I hope we see each other soon.

Best regards,

[signature]

MGM Studios
Boreham Wood
Herts
England

Letter from Stanley Kubrick to Satyajit Ray, 9 May 1967

Envelope and letter from the renowned cinematographer Haskell Wexler to Satyajit Ray

Dear Mr Ray:

I am very sorry to have missed seeing you before you left the States.

I am afraid my phone conversation said very little of what I would like to say.

Anyway please know I am available and would be honored to work for you on any film without pay.

After this Steve McQueen picture I will only work on projects of my own or with directors whose philosophy of life has meaning for me.

Please call on me.

Best regards,

Haskell Wexler

Excerpt from the GUARDIAN
16 May 1967

ALIEN IN A LOTUS POND — SATYAJIT RAY talks to ANDREW CAVE

Satyajit Ray lives in a modest top-floor flat in a middleclass district of Calcutta. The director of the *Pather Panchali* trilogy and of *Charulata*—films that many people think among the finest made since the war—works by choice for an industry so narrowly based on the West Bengal public as to bring uncertain rewards. After a period of frustration he is now in full spate again; he looks forward to directing Peter Sellers (as an Indian in an Indian setting) in *The Alien*, an original script of Ray's to which he has given a touch of science fiction.

When I saw Ray in London four years ago he was wearing an international film director's uniform—suede shoes, fawn trousers, the lot. In Calcutta, he wears the "jama-kapor" (loose white shirt and dhoti) and looks more comfortable. ...

"Bengali films are in crisis," he says. "The problem is distribution. There is very little public for them outside West Bengal—and now the West Bengal audience has developed a taste for Hindi films. You see them queuing outside cinemas that show Bombay films—well, it's understandable. These films deliberately show all sorts of exotic backgrounds—Japan, Switzerland; one film recently took you up to the Eiffel Tower—but still broke off for an Indian song and dance... Besides there are some very pretty girls in Bombay."

The crisis has had two effects on Ray's work. First, it dried up finance for a film he had planned on a famous children's story by his grandfather. He also concluded that in future he should work on a more international scale, still based on Bengal ("I could never work in Bombay"), but with more English dialogue and some English-speaking actors. Hence *The Alien* (or, as it will be known in India, *Avatar*).

"It is a science fiction only in a superficial way. There is a spaceship in it—it lands in a lotus pond in the Birbhum district in Bengal."

"Only the top shows—the local people think it may be a temple miraculously growing out of the pond. Inside the spaceship is an alien creature, a little like a refugee child perhaps, who comes out only at night and works miracles—brings water for the crops, or makes mangoes grow overnight. In the district there is a Marwari (North Indian) business man who is sinking tubewells, as a benefaction but with a little bit of an eye to profit, an American who is sinking them for him, some santals (tribesmen) with a little chapel and a padre. The story has a lot of ramifications—social, political, religious."

He is clear about some of his targets. "You know, at a certain age men who have made a lot of money in business, by one means or another start thinking of spiritual things and spending a lot of money on good works. There was a group of temples in Birbhum district—Bengali Terracotta temples, partly ruined, very beautiful; I had often thought of shooting a scene there. The last time I went there to see them they had been completely covered in plaster, and painted pink. Pink!" He smiles.

The Marwari will be Peter Sellers. About his ability as actor and mimic Ray is enthusiastic. "In the film he will speak English most of the time, but he will also speak Bengali to the Bengali characters—in a Marwari accent... It's extraordinary, he was in India during the war and picked it all up—he can speak English in a UP accent, a South Indian accent. Well, just now and then his Bengali accent sounds like a little South Indian—but all he needs to get it right is a few pointers."

Because of Sellers's commitments, *The Alien* can start shooting only in December. Meanwhile, Ray is finishing shooting on *Chiriyakhana*, a thriller ("for home consumption only"), which his assistants had started and which they asked him to come in on when he was at a loose end. After that he intends to make, this time on his own, *Asani Sanket* (*The Distant Thunder*), a story of the Bengal famine of 1943 by Bibhutibhusan Banerjee, the author of the novel on which the *Pather Panchali* trilogy was based. As in the trilogy, Soumitra Chatterjee will play the lead.

Excerpt from LOS ANGELES TIMES
12 June 1967

INDIAN MOVIEMAKER'S IMPLAUSIBLE INGREDIENTS
by KEVIN THOMAS, Times Staff Writer

Sunken treasure, science fiction and Peter Sellers—none of these sounds like the ingredients for a film by Satyajit Ray, India's foremost director, who won worldwide acclaim with his Apu Trilogy—*Pather Panchali, Aparajito* and *The World of Apu*—which followed the life and times of a Bengali boy from childhood to manhood.

But they are. Ray's first international production will be called *The Alien* and will be filmed in India for a Columbia release. Sellers, who will be the first major Western star to work for a major Asian director, plays a rich Bengali merchant who mistakes a space capsule for a sacred temple and decides to restore it.

As for that treasure, some of the 3 tons of mint 1702 Muslim silver coins that Ray's producer, Ceylon-based film-maker and former professional diver, Michael Wilson, discovered five years off the Great Basses Reef will be used to back the venture.

Before the 1956 Cannes Festival, in which *Pather Panchali* had been entered, the Indian cinema had been as unknown as the Japanese prior to *Rashomon*. Since then, Ray, who has now made 14 films, has been ranked among the world's great directors, but the Indian film industry, second only to the Japanese in output, remains isolated, still devoted to escapist fantasies of ethnic appeal.

At 46, Calcutta-born Ray is a tall, good-looking man who sounds like George Sanders. A one-time commercial artist, he made *Pather Panchali* in his spare time with a largely non-professional cast and crew and eventually completed it with grants from the West Bengal government. He has composed the music for his last six pictures and did the score for James Ivory's *Shakespeare Wallah*.

At 32, bearded, slim Mike Wilson makes an ideal partner to the unassuming, intellectual Ray, combining an astute knowledge and appreciation of Ray's movies with a sharp business sense.

It was Wilson who got the project under way. A long-time partner in underwater exploration with the distinguished science fiction writer and aerospace authority, Arthur C. Clarke, he came up with the idea of combining the talents of Clarke and Ray, who has been a science fiction addict since his teens. (Later, Ray found out he would not need Clarke's expertise for *The Alien* which he is writing himself.) Then Wilson thought of Sellers, whom he and Ray conferred with in Paris last April. Sellers had never seen a Ray film, says Wilson, but was sold when he was shown *Charulata*.

"*The Alien* tells what happens when a space capsule descends upon a lotus pond in a small Bengali village. It will be a film with social, religious and metaphysical implications. It's a parable with many levels of meaning."

PERFECT ACCENT

"No Indian audience would accept an India actor as a Marwari," says Ray. "Also, Peter can simulate the Indian accent perfectly. He spent a year in Calcutta while in the service and played an Indian in *The Millionairess* and now is playing another in *The Party*."

"And Sellers has insured foreign backing yet Satyajit is allowed full artistic control," adds Wilson forthrightly.

As he and Ray outline the allegorical plot—which won't be revealed here—it becomes clear that this movie will not after all be a departure for Ray, whose movies tend to be quests for some kind of spiritual truth and frequently have heroes who struggle in vain for control over destinies of those who are dependent upon them as well as their own.

That title *The Alien* refers to various individuals and groups—Sellers and the ruling class to which he belongs, and American engineer (not yet cast) in his employ, the inhabitant of the capsule and a group of natives cut off from the rest of the world, the Santals.

The Alien has by no means been Ray's first chance at Hollywood, which he first visited first nine years ago. "Selznick offered me carte blanche for a film in India— provided there would be a part for Jennifer Jones," recalls Ray with a smile. ...

"I find I now favor films over directors. There are so many disappointments. I think the heyday for Hollywood has passed. There's the occasional splendid thing of course—something from Kubrick or Frankenheimer. Or maybe Kazan.

"I don't think I could ever work here myself. It's too foreign for me. The number of people on a set terrifies me. I never work with a crew of more than six and seven people."

Yet with Hollywood backing, Satyajit Ray, whose films since the Apu Trilogy have received little or no distribution in the United States, may with *The Alien* reach an audience greater than that for all his previous pictures. "Fireworks are always spectacular," says Mike Wilson, comparing his own adventuresome life to Ray's calm, even development as a director. "But it's the steady flame that survives."

Excerpt from the NEW YORK TIMES
25 June 1967

FOR RAY, A FAMINE AND A FAIRY TALE
by A.H. Weiler

... Ray's third project, *The Alien*, starring Peter Sellers, will be filmed in October, 1968, in a village about 100 miles from Calcutta. "I hope to show," says Ray, "the conflicts among three forces—man's present wants, ancient Indian traditions and the space age of the future."

India's Movie Maker To Accept Challenge

By BOB THOMAS
HOLLYWOOD (AP) — Can a

SATYAJIT RAY

...nous India Producer ...king Film In English

BOB THOMAS
WOOD (AP) — Can a
film maker translate
to a language that is
not his own?
was an accomplished
spectacular success by Ita-
chelangelo Antonioni in
first English-language film,
p." Less successful has
France's Francois Truf-
whose "Fahrenheit 451"
to move the critics. Nor
English-made films of
Polanski drawn the
of those he made in

foreign directors such
's Ingmar Bergman and
's Federico Fellini
so far resisted the
at the bigger, English-
ant famous film maker
, plans to accept the

Other directors such as
Sweden's Ingmar Bergman
Italy's...
resisted the...
bigger,...
But Saty...

chali," "Aparajito" "The World
of Apu" — made him a winner
of film festivals. After 14 movies he seeks a new challenge.
"In most of my films I have
been working with nonactors."
Ray and Producer Michael
Wilson figure they have their
virtuoso in Peter Sellers, who
has agreed to appear in "The
Alien" on the basis of Ray's
reputation; the actor didn't
even need to see the script. Now
Ray and Wilson are seeking an

Said he: "Bombay has its own
make-believe world."
The world of Satyajit Ray instead reflects the soul and heart
of India, and that accounts for
the fact that he is the only Indian film maker to be recognized outside the country's borders.

Indian Film Maker Accepts Hollywood

By BOB THOMAS
HOLLYWOOD, Calif. (AP) —
Can a masterful film maker
translate his genius to a language that is not his own?
The feat was accomplished
with spectacular success by
Italy's Michelangelo Antonioni
in his first English-language
film, "Blow-up." Less successful has been France's
Francois Truffaut, whose

Wilson figure they have their
virtuoso in Peter Sellers, who
has agreed to appear in "The
Alien" on the basis of Ray's
reputation; the actor didn't
even need to see the script.
Now Ray and Wilson...

scornfully of the product of
Bombay, which is "100 per

LAUDERDALE ADM. $1.00
DRIVE IN THEATRE
So RICHARD AT 27th AVE.

dates. Glick believes that th
census findings will speed th
process of "judicious mate s
lection" and that it will go b
yond this to help husbands a
wives maintain "an optim
relationship after marriag
He suggests that the term "m
riage quotient" will come
usage. If you are already
ried, your marriage quot
would be the probability rev
ed in the tables that ma
couples similar to yours are
maining married "until d

India Producer Plans English Language Film

By BOB THOMAS
AP Movie-Television Writer
HOLLYWOOD (AP) — Can a
masterful film maker translate
his genius to a language that is
not his own?
The feat was accomplished
with spectacular success by Italy's Michelangelo Antonioni in
his first English-language film,
"Blow-up." Less successful has
been France's Francois Truffaut, whose "Fahrenheit 451"
failed to move the critics. Nor
have the English-made films of
Roman Polanski drawn the
plaudits of those he made in
Poland.
Other foreign directors such
as Sweden's Ingmar Bergman
and Italy's Federico Fellini
have so far resisted the offers
to aim at the bigger, English-
speaking market. But Satyajit
Ray, most famous film maker
of India, plans to accept the
challenge.
Ray has been visiting Hollywood to make plans for "The
Alien" which he will make for
Columbia Pictures. Until now,
all of his movies have been
filmed in the Bengali Language,
primarily for the Indian audience.
The appeal of his films has
extended beyond his country's
borders, attracting international
attention to Indian films for the
first time. His trilogy of the life
of a village boy — "Pather Panchali," "Aparajito," "The World
of Apu" made him a winner
of film festivals. After 14 mov-

ies he seeks a new challenge.
"In most of my films I have
been working with nonactors,"
he remarked. "Now I want to
see what it is like to work with
virtuoso performers."
Ray and Producer M
Wilson figure they have
virtuoso in Peter Sellers
has agreed to appear in
Alien" on the basis of
reputation; the actor
even need to see the scr
Ray and Wilson are see
American actor for the
major role. They wo
Steve McQueen or Marl
do, but then, what film
wouldn't?
Ray continues to wor
cutta, which he desc
"the center for mode
usually based on nov
short stories and roo
environment of In
speaks rather scorn
product of Bombay,
"100 per cent commerc
big budgets and colo
Said he: "Bombay
m ke believe world."
The world of Saty
stead reflects the so
of India, and that
the fact that he is
d an film maker to
n ed outside the c
ders.

Indian Director Plans English Language Movie

By BOB THOMAS

AP Movie-Television Writer
HOLLYWOOD (AP) — Can a
masterful film maker translate his
genius to a language that is [not]
his own?
The feat w...
spec...

maker of India, pla...
challenge.
Ray has been vis...
to make plans fo...
which he will mak...
Pictures. Until n...
movies have been...
Bengali 'anguage,...
th. audience.

al of hi...
nd his...
ting in...
'ndian

His t...
age bo...
'Apara...

SATYAJIT RAY

FOUR — THE DAILY MAIL, Hagerstown, Md.
Monday, June 26, 1967

Masterful Film Maker Works In Any Language

By BOB THOMAS
AP Movie-Television Writer
HOLLYWOOD (AP) — Can a
masterful film maker translate
his genius to a language that is
not his own?
The feat was accomplished
with spectacular success by Italy's Michelangelo Antonioni in
first English-language film,
"..." Less successful has
...Truf- ...the Indian au-

of India, plans to accept the
challenge.
Ray has been visiting Hollywood to make plans for "the
Alien," which he will make for
Columbia Pictures. Until now,
all of his movies have been
filmed in the Bengali Language,
primarily for the Indian audience.
The appeal of his films has
extended beyond his country's
borders, attracting international
... to Indian films for the
... story of the Pan-

Other...
Swed...
Italy's...
resisted...
bigger,...
But Sat...

THE BATTLE CREEK ENQUIRER AND NEWS

No Speaka Da English!
Foreign Film Directors Lose in Translation

...WOOD (AP) —Can a
...l film maker translate
...us to a language that is
...wn?
...feat was accomplished
...ectacular success by Ita-
...chelangelo Antonioni in
... English-language film,
...p." Less successful has
...rance's Francois Truf-
...hose "Fahrenheit 451"
... move the critics. Nor
... English-made films of
... Polanski drawn the
... of those he made in

... foreign directors such
...s Ingmar Bergman and
...Federico Fellini have so
...isted the offers to aim at
...igger, English-speaking
... But Satyajit Ray, most
... film maker of India,
...o accept the challenge.
...has been visiting Holly-
...to make plans for "The
...' ll make for

all of his movies have been
filmed in the Bengali Language,
primarily for the Indian audience.
The appeal of his films has
extended beyond his country's
borders, attracting international
attention to Indian films for the
first time. His trilogy of the life
of a village boy — "Pather Panchali," "Aparajito," "The World
of Apu" — made him a winner
of film festivals. After 14 movies he seeks a new challenge.
"In most of my films I have
been working with nonactors,"
he remarked. "Now I want to
see what it is like to work with
virtuoso performers."
Ray and Producer Michael
Wilson figure they have their
virtuoso in Peter Sellers, who
has agreed to appear in "The
Alien" on the basis of Ray's
reputation; the actor didn't
even need to see the script. Now
Ray and Wilson are seeking an

major role. They would like
Steve McQueen or Marlon Brando, but then, what film maker
wouldn't?
Ray is a surprisingly tall man
of 46 years, with luxuriant black
hair and large, sad eyes. He
speaks in flawless, British-accented English and seems happiest when he is talking about
films. He was a founder of the
Calcutta Film Society and
moonlighted from an advertising job to film "Pather Panchali."
"I was shooting it during
parts of three years," he said.
"At one time the whole project
was shelved for eight months
because I couldn't find any
more money. Finally the government took over financing of
the film as a cultural venture."
The wary Indian didn't quit
his advertising job until after
"pather Panchali" had been
released and begun to attract
ders

Ray continues to work in Calcutta, which he describes as
"the center for modest films,
usually based on novels and
short stories and rooted in the
environment of India." He
speaks rather scornfully of the
product of Bombay, which is
"100 per cent commercial, with
big budgets and color."
Said he: "Bombay has its own
make-believe world."
The world of Satyajit Ray instead reflects the soul and heart
of India, and that accounts for
the fact that he is the only Indian film maker to be recognized outside the country's borders.

Indian Produ...

By BOB THOMAS

HOLLYWOOD (AP)—Can a masterful film maker
his genius to a language that is not his own?
The feat was accomplished with spectacular su
Italy's Michelangelo Antonioni in his first Englis
film "Blow-up." Less successful has been France's
Truffaut, whose "Farneheit 451" failed to move th
Nor have the English-made films of Roman Polanski d
plaudits of those he made in Poland.
Other foreign directors such as Sweden's Ingmar
and Italy's Federico Fellini have so far resisted. But
to aim at the bigger, English-speaking market. But
Ray, most famous film maker of India, plans to ac
challenge.

★ ★ ★

RAY HAS BEEN VISITING Hollywood to lay
"The Alien," which he will make for Columbia Pi
now, all of his movies have been filmed in the Bengali
primarily for the Indian audience.
The appeal of his films has extended beyond his
borders, attracting international attention to Indian
the first time. His trilogy of the life of a village boy,
Panchali," "Aparaji," "The World of Apu"—made
winner of film festivals. After 14 movies, he seek
challenge

reputation; the actor didn't
even need to see the script. Now
... and Wilson are seeking an
... american actor for the other
... ajor role. They would like
... teve McQueen or Marlon Bran-
... but then, what film maker

SATYAJIT RAY
Indian Film Maker Plans U.S. Debut

By BOB THOMAS
AP Movie-Television Writer

HOLLYWOOD (AP) — Can a masterful film maker translate his genius to a language that is not his own?

The feat was accomplished with spectacular success by Italy's Michelangelo Antonioni in his first English-language film, "Blow-up." Less successful has been France's Francois Truf-

Sweden's Ingmar Bergman and Italy's Federico Fellini have so far resisted the offers to aim at the bigger, English-speaking market. But Satyajit Ray, most famous film maker of India, plans to accept the challenge.

Ray has been visiting Hollywood to make plans for "The Alien," which he will make for Columbia Pictures. Until now, all of his movies have been filmed in the Bengali Language, the Indian au-

PLANS MOVIE IN HOLLYWOOD
Famous Director Of India To Accept Film Challenge

By BOB THOMAS

HOLLYWOOD (AP) — Can a masterful film maker translate his genius to a language that is not his own?

The appeal of his films has extended beyond his country's borders, attracting inte-

cented English and seem

Masterful Movie ... Translate Genius?

By BOB THOMAS
... Movie-Television Writer

...D (AP) — Can a masterful film maker ... us to a language that is not his own?

...accomplished ...ecess by Ita-...Antonioni in ...cessful has ...ancois Truf-...renheit 451" ...critics. Nor ...made the in ...drawn the ...made in

...ectors such ...ar Bergman ...erica Fellini ...of the offers ...ger, English-...But Satyajit ...film maker ...accept th

more money. Finally the government took over financing of the film as a cultural venture."

The wary Indian didn't quit his advertising job until after "pather Panchali" had been released and began to attract attention.

Ray continues to work in Calcutta, which he describes as "the center for modest films, usually based on novels and short stories and rooted in the environment of India." He speaks rather scornfully of the product of Bombay, which is "100 per cent commercial, with big budgets and color."

Said he: "Bombay has its own make-believe world."

...of my films I have ...g with nonactors," ...d. "Now I want to ...is like to work with ...formers."

Producer Michael ...re they have their ...Peter Sellers, who ...to appear in "The ...the basis of Ray's ...the actor didn't ...o see the script. Now ...ilson are seeking an ...ctor for the other ...e. They would like ...teen or Marlon Bran-...en, what film maker

surprisingly tall man ..., with luxuriant black ...large, sad eyes. He ...flawless, British-ac-...glish and seems hap-

---

To Direct English Movie
India's Famed Film Maker Accepting New Challenge

By BOB THOMAS

HOLLYWOOD (AP) — Can a masterful film maker translate his genius to a language that is not his own?

The feat was accomplished with spectacular success by Italy's Michelangelo Antonioni in his first English-language film, "Blow-up." Less successful has been France's Francois Truf-faut, whose "Fahrenheit 451" failed to move the critics. Nor have the English-made films of Roman Polanski drawn the plaudits of those he made in Poland.

Other foreign directors such as Sweden's Ingmar Bergman and Italy's Federico Fellini have so far resisted the offers to aim at the bigger, English-speaking market. But Satyajit Ray, most famous film maker of India, plans to accept the challenge.

Now In Hollywood

Ray has been visiting Hollywood to make plans for "The Alien," which he will make for Columbia Pictures. Until now, all of his movies have been filmed in the Bengali language, primarily for the Indian audience.

The appeal of his films has extended beyond his country's borders, attracting international attention to Indian films for the first time. His trilogy of the life of a village boy — "Pather Pan-

chali," "Aparajito," "The World of Apu" — made him a winner of film festivals. After 14 movies he seeks a new challenge.

"In most of my films I have been working with nonactors," he remarked. "Now I want to see what it is like to work with virtuoso performers."

Get Peter Sellers

Ray and Producer Michael Wilson figure they have their virtuoso in Peter Sellers, who has agreed to appear in "The Alien" on the basis of Ray's reputation; the actor didn't even need to see the script. Now Ray and Wilson are seeking an American actor for the other major role. They would like Steve McQueen or Marlon Brando, but then, what film maker wouldn't?

Ray continues to work in Calcutta, which he describes as "the center for modest films, usually based on novels and short stories and rooted in the environment of India." He speaks rather scornfully of the product of Bombay, which is "100 per cent commercial, with big budgets and color."

Said he: "Bombay has its own make-believe world."

The world of Satyajit Ray instead reflects the soul and heart of India, and that accounts for the fact that he is the only Indian film maker to be recognized outside the country's bor-ders.

SATYAJIT RAY, most famous film maker o discusses plans in Hollywood for his first English movie, "The Alien." In making the movie for Pictures, starring Peter Sellers, he will attempt to his genius into a language not his own. All of movies have been filmed in the Bengali language for the Indian audience. (AP

Indian Film Director Trys English Movie

By BOB THOMAS
AP Movie-Television Writer

HOLLYWOOD (AP) — Can a masterful film maker translate his genius to a language that is not his own?

The feat was accomplished with spectacular success by Italy's Michelangelo Antonioni in his first English-language film, "Blow-up." Less successful has been France's Francois Truf-

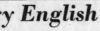

India's Famed Film Maker Tries Moving His Genius To Holly...

By BOB THOMAS
AP Movie-Television Writer

HOLLYWOOD (AP) — Can a ...ly's M...

The feat was accomplished of Apu" — made him a winner with sp...

Steve McQueen do, but then, wouldn...

ms I have nonactors," I wa

Indian Film Mogul Eyes New Heights

By BOB THOMAS
AP Movie-Television Writer

HOLLYWOOD (AP) — Can a masterful film maker translate his genius to a language that is not his own?

The feat was accomplished with spectacular success by Italy's Michelangelo Antonioni in his first English-language film, "Blow-up." Less successful has

---

Indian To Try Translating Film Genius

By BOB THOMAS

HOLLYWOOD (AP) — Can a masterful film maker translate his genius to a language that is not his own?

The feat was accomplished with spectacular success by Italy's Michelangelo Antonioni in his first English-language film, "Blow-up." Less successful has been France's Francois Truffaut, whose "Fahrenheit 451" failed to move the critics. Nor have the English-made films of Roman Polanski drawn the plaudits of those he made in Poland.

Other foreign directors such as Sweden's Ingmar Bergman and Italy's Federico Fellini have so far resisted the offers to aim at the bigger, English-speaking market. But Satyajit Ray, most famous film maker of India, plans to accept the challenge.

Ray has been visiting Holly-wood to lay plans for "The

has agreed to appear in "The Alien" on the basis of Ray's reputation; the actor didn't even need to see the script. Now Ray and Wilson are seeking an American actor for the other major role. They would like Steve McQueen or Marlon Brando, but then, what film maker wouldn't?

Ray is a surprisingly tall man of 46 years, with luxuriant black hair and large, sad eyes. He speaks in flawless, British-accented English and seems happiest when he is talking about film. He was a founder of the Calcutta Film Society and moonlighted his advertising job to film "Pather Pan-chali."

"I WAS SHOOTING it during parts of three years," he said. "At one time the whole project was shelved for eight months because I couldn't find any more money. Finally, the

---

Director Found for 'Alien'

By BOB THOMAS (AP)

HOLLYWOOD (AP) masterful film maker ...his genius to a la... not his own?

The feat ...with spectac... ly's Michel... his first... "Blow-up... been fa... faut, w...

seeking an the other would like

Excerpt from the NEW YORK TIMES
21 May 1967

PETER SELLERS IS ONE-MAN BAND
by A.H. WEILER

...Last but certainly not least of Sellers's revelations was that he has teamed with India's top director, Satyajit Ray, to make *The Alien*. This, he hinted vaguely, "is based on a novel by Arthur C. Clarke who worked with Stanley Kubrick on his new *Odyssey 2001* film. Kubrick, he and I are good friends and we've talked about it with Ray. All I can say about it now is that it's a science-fiction story set in Calcutta. It's not comic at all but very serious business and I'll play a very serious Calcutta businessman who becomes involved in a complicated science-fiction affair."...

Excerpt from the SYDNEY MORNING HERALD
19 August 1967

SELLERS IN THE ROLE OF A PHILOSOPHER
by RODERICK MANN in London

..."However, I am doing something rather interesting after this film. I'm playing the part of a Bengali businessman in an Indian film *The Alien*, to be made by the great Indian director Satyajit Ray.

"I think I'm the first European actor ever to play the part of an Indian in a major Indian production. It'll be a straight part. Satyajit Ray saw me playing the Indian doctor in *The Millionairess* and decided I could do it. It seems I'm on a bit of an Indian kick at the moment. In *The Party* I play an Indian student..."

Excerpt from HONOLULU STAR BULLETIN
Sunday, 1 October 1967

HOLLYWOOD'N EVERYWHERE
by SHEILAH GRAHAM

...The picture Peter Sellers will make in India with director Satyajit Ray, will have most of the dialogue in Bengali, with subtitles in English. It's called *The Alien* and is described as a science-fiction story with mystical overtones. Very much Peter's cup of tea...

Excerpt from LOS ANGELES TIMES
19 October 1967

...Peter Sellers has returned to Hollywood for pre-production work on his next assignment, *I Love You, Alice B. Toklas!* at Warner's Seven Arts. The one after that will take him to India in late spring, not for meditation, but for direction by India's renowned Satyajit Ray. I wonder who'll come out on top in that teaming madcap— extrovert Sellers or mystical, introspective Satyajit Ray? ...

Excerpt from DES MOINES TRIBUNE
1 November 1967

SHEILAH GRAHAM (North American newspaper Alliance)
London, England

...Mr Coburn will be going to India, but not to meditate there except on his own private time. He is planning a picture with Satyajit Ray. It is titled *The Alien*, will co-star Peter Sellers and will be shot in Calcutta. ...

Excerpt from PITTSBURGH POST GAZETTE
6 November 1967

SHEILAH GRAHAM (North American newspaper Alliance)
London, England

...The first international movie for Satyajit Ray, the brilliant Indian director, will be *The Alien* with James Coburn and Peter Sellers...

Excerpt from the TIMES, London
4 October 1967

SELLERS UNDER THE GREAT RAY

India's leading film director Satyajit Ray had seen more than a dozen Peter Sellers films when he cast him as an Indian businessman in *The Alien*, a science-fiction fantasy he is to make for Columbia Pictures next year: but *The Millionairess*, in which Sellers played an Indian doctor, was not among them.

"I chose Sellers because I couldn't think of any Indian actor who could play the part," says Ray, who is in London to discuss the film with producer Mike Wilson. "It demands a highly experienced professional and Sellers has a face that needs only a little make-up to become Indian."

Ray (pronounced "Rye") had the idea for *The Alien* three years ago. A science fiction addict (he is president of the S.F. Cine Club in Calcutta) he wrote the script after talking the story over with S.F. novelist Arthur C. Clarke. "It's about an extra-terrestrial spaceship, which has a poetic interior that is almost a living organism."

A tall, powerfully built and handsome man of 45, Ray's almost perfect English has none of the "Bombay Welsh" of a Sellers's Indian. He has not previously made a film with English dialogue—and at least 40 percent of *The Alien* will be in his native Bengali.

He says he is feeling his way around to doing "a wholly English-language film".

"Four years ago I discussed doing *A Passage to India* with Forster, but I couldn't work on an out-and-out English subject. I might do a film about Indians in London if I could find a story. I'd also like to tackle the Indian Mutiny."

Before grappling with *The Alien*, which will be filmed in a village outside his hometown, Calcutta, from October to December next year, Ray is to make his sixteenth wholly Indian feature—a musical fantasy based on a children's story told by his grandfather.

PETER SELLERS

December 13, 1967

In the year of 1967 and in the month of December
An auspicious month coming as it does at the end of the year
And not the slightest alike to November
Is a month that I will long remember.

I received one day
From Satyajit Ray
Information I required without delay
So that I could say to my friends the evening of that day
The film you are about to see is the first film of a trilogy
And is called "The Ballad of the Road"
Or "Pather Panchali"
And in it there is contained a scene in which is depicted
Two children sitting in a field of barley
Watching a train go by
Under an azure sky
So beautiful you feel that you want to die.

Anyway, as I was saying,
Mr. Peter Sellers by whom it was received
Has achieved fame in his own peculiar way
By watching the faces of his friends that day
In their reverie travelling along the ballad of the road.

Sincerely

Peter.

Letter from Peter Sellers to Satyajit Ray, 13 December 1967

Brando and Ray

Ray and Marlon Brando having a conversation while Madhur Jaffrey looks on
Right Page: Telegram from Marlon Brando to Mike Wilson, 7 September 1967

A958 LA474

LLC282 INTL TDL BEVERLY HILLS CALIF 98 1/50 6 354P PDT

WS   89

T MIKE WILSON

LONDON HILTON LONDON@ (ENGLAND)

REGRET THAT AT THE TIME YOU WERE CALLING I WAS HITHER WHILST

OU WERE YON IN ADDITION I WAS IN THE MIDST OF A MOST UNCOMFORTABLE

ND DISTRESSING SITUATION MY DIVORCE I KNOW I MUST HAVE CAUSED

OU SOME INCONVENIENCE AND APOLOGIZE IF

END 1

LLC282 2/48

OSSIBLE I WOULD CERTAINLY APPRECIATE READING MR RAYS SCRIPT

ND WOULD BE MOST PLEASED IF YOU COULD SEND IT TO ME IN LOSANGELES

IT IS TOO LATE AGAIN MY SINCERE APOLOGIES FOR ANY TROUBLE

MIGHT HAVE CAUSED MY BEST TO MR RAY SINCERELY YOURS

MARLON BRANDO.

INDIAN POSTS AND TELEGRAPHS DEPARTMENT

TELEGRAM 10037

Address

SATYAJIT RAY 3 LAKETEMPLEROAD

CALCUTTA29BENGAL

Time of { Booking _____
         { Receipt _____

From _____

By _____

The sequence of entries at the beginning of this telegram is—class of telegram, time handed in, serial number, office of origin, date, service instructions (if any) and number of words.

This form must accompany any enquiry respecting this telegram.

A. T. Press. Cal. 9. 8DP/L-511/Ptg. 66, dated 2-2-67—20,000 Bks.

FIRST FOLD

= XF 531P PST CR 289 BEVERLY HILLS CALIF 15 OCS 81

= MR DEAR SATYAJIT I HAVE RECEIVED YOUR LETTER FOR WHICH I THANK YOU VERY MUCH

AND BELIEVE ME I LOOK FORWARD EAGERLY TO FILMING THE ALIEN WITH YOU STOP I HAVE

JUST COMMENCED PRINCIPLE PHOTOGRAPHY ON MY NEW MOVIE SO PLEASE FORGIVE ME IF I

DONT WRITE A LETTER TO YOU FOR FEW WEEKS STOP I AM RATHER HARRASED AH LINES AND

PLAYING A DIFFICULT CHARACTER STOP I WILL WRITE SOON VERY SINCERELY =

PETER SELLERS =

Telegram from Peter Sellers to Satyajit Ray, 16 November 1967

LAW OFFICES

LOUIS C. BLAU

Louis C. Blau
Bruce M. Stiglitz
Paul Gutman
Stanley Belkin
Sidney A. Copilow

9777 WILSHIRE BOULEVARD

BEVERLY HILLS, CALIFORNIA 90212

CRestview 3-0864·TRemont 8-5660

CABLE ADDRESS
"BLAULAW"
Telex No. 677226

February 14, 1968

Mr. Satyajit Ray
3 Lake Temple Road
Calcutta 29
India

Dear Satyajit:

Thought you would be interested in a review of your film
"Big City" which appeared in the Los Angeles Times last week.

I received a letter from Michael Wilson which I have not
yet answered. I would appreciate it if you would write to him
and ask him to send you a copy of the letter or authorize me to
do so. After you receive the copy, you and Michael and I will
have to agree on what I am to ask of Columbia. Obviously it
would be most unwise for the project if I went to Columbia and
literally asked for everything that is contained in Mike's letter.

It is most important that you stay in communication with
Peter Sellers, who is presently at Warner Bros. studios shooting
his picture, "I Love You, Alice B. Toklas". Also, let me know
exactly what your contact has been with Peter and what responses
you have received from him.

I am aware of the visit of the representative of Columbia
Pictures England to India and the favorable report he made upon
his return to London. Have you had any further word from London?

Kindest regards,

LOUIS C. BLAU

LCB:dcr

Enclosure

Letter from Louis C. Blau (attorney and film lawyer) to Satyajit Ray, 14 February 1968

PETER SELLERS

c/o R.D.A. Wills
16, Rue du Roveray
1207 Geneva
Switzerland
February 16, 1968

Mr. Satyajit Ray
3 Lake Temple Road
Calcutta 29
Bengal, India

Dear Satyajit:

A few days ago, Blake Edwards and I did some retakes for a scene
in the film, "The Party" which you may remember we were shooting
when you were last out here approximately six months ago. The
object of the retake was to shorten the scene in the playing which
was over-long and insufficiently covered, thus rendering it
impossible for the editor to condense it. However, "to cut a
long story short", begging your pardon, I exclaimed during
one part of the retake 'Hare Ram Ram' and I now remember that
this expression was contained in your script, "The Alien" and
that you had asked me not to use it anywhere else.

I am truly very sorry indeed about this Satyajit because I am
certain that the Mirisch Company will use the retake. I feel
I have broken a promise to you which is something I always try
to avoid and I sincerely hope you will accept my apology and
that what I have done will not spoil our future relationship and
rapport.

Kindest regards.

Sincerely,

Peter Sellers

PS:mg

Columbia (British)
Productions Limited

ST. MARGARET'S HOUSE, 19/23, WELLS STREET, LONDON, W.1

26th March, 1968.

Mr. Satyajit Ray,
3 Lake Temple Road,
Calcutta 29,
<u>INDIA.</u>

Dear Satyajit,

I shall try and deal with the points you raised in your letters of 14th and 21st March as far as possible.

I have written to Bill Wills regarding a start date for Peter Sellers. Columbia (British) are quite happy to go along with your wishes to commence shooting in January 1969.

I had recorded here your wish regarding your credit for the screenplay, namely that it would be along the lines of "Screenplay by Satyajit Ray with acknowledgements to Michael J. Wilson". Again, we are happy to go along with your wishes on this.

Regarding the part of Devlin, I have discussed this with Max Setton. He has asked me to give you the following list of names:

MARLON BRANDO
BURT LANCASTER
LEE MARVIN
STEVE MCQUEEN
GEORGE SEGAL
ROBERT MITCHAM
RICHARD WIDMARK
JAMES GARNER
WARREN BEATTY
ARTHUR KENNEDY
PAUL NEWMAN

He would like to have a choice of three of these in your order of preference, and he suggests that you write a personal note to each selected one, asking whether he would be interested in making the film with you. Max feels that your reputation might pursuade one or two of these to

cont./

- 2 -   26th March, 1968.

make a reasonable deal. If you let us know your preference, we will follow up from our end. I am sorry no one had communicated with you earlier regarding this. I have also heard that Coburn might be prepared to make a reasonable deal now that the film will almost certainly be shot in 1969.

The Michael Wilson situation is rather complex. The basis of the contract sent to you was an Agreement between Indus Productions and ourselves dated July 13th 1967. In the absence of detailed knowledge of the conditions of your association with Indus Productions and Michael Wilson, it is difficult for us to help. The Agreement of July 13th 1967 specifically names Michael Wilson as the individual Producer, and he was paid certain advances in salary. The sum of £10,000 on account of your services in writing the original screenplay was included in a bank draft of £15,000, payable to Indus. It was specifically stated in this Agreement that the advance was to be on account of your writing costs. I can only suggest that you ask Blau to take whatever possible action to recover this sum from Mike, as our present Agreement is with Indus. In other words, the disposal of the money is between Indus, Wilson and yourself. The bank draft was handed to Michael Wilson on 8th August 1967.

Once the contract is completed, the rights of the story will be owned by Columbia (British) Productions Ltd. Louis Blau has been asked some considerable time ago for the chain of title documents, but has not yet replied. The question of an acknowledgement of receipt of a sum which has not been paid to you can only really be sorted when we know what Indus Productions did with the payment we made to them.

The delay in straightening out the situation is regrettable. Ken Maidment informs me that your suggestion of £50,000 over a two year period with the remainder as an advance against a feature film of your own choice, which Columbia will own and exploit, is basically acceptable to him in principle.

I am leaving for Turkey on a survey tomorrow, and will be away for about two weeks. I will write again on my return.

Kindest regards,

Sincerely,

Nuk

pp D.C.R. MACDONALD

cc: Mr. M. Setton
    Mr. K. L. Maidment
    Mr. J. Van Eyssen
    Mr. R. E. Atkinson
    Mr. A. E. Stroud
    Mr. L. C. Blau

Letter from D.C.R. MacDonald
(Columbia UK) to Satyajit Ray,
26 March 1968

Satyajit Ray

3 Lake Temple Road, Calcutta 29   April 9, 1968

Mr D C R Macdonald
c/o Columbia British Productions Ltd
St Margaret's House
19/23 Wells Street, London.

Dear Nick:

Mike Wilson turned up here suddenly last week, and we
had several encounters. When I asked him about the
$10,000, he first of all denied having received it, then
said it was actually a loan designated as screen advance
against the screenplay for reasons of accountancy, and
finally hinted that since Columbia wouldn't reimburse
him for all the expenses he had to incur for my sake, he
had used up the money to meet them. All of which led to
a final and definite parting of ways. I am not tied to
Mike by any sort of agreement. Columbia have signed an
agreement with Indus, but Indus doesn't own the story,
nor does it own my services as director. The rest is up to
Blau, I suppose.

Peter wrote from Switzerland in answer to my letter to say
that January would suit him for The Alien. Since then I
have received a cable from him asking me to confirm the
start date, which I have sent.

I don't know if you'd find the enclosed clipping as
alarming as I do, but if theParty is anything like what
the piece says, it won't help our project. I watched the
shooting in Hollywood and was troubled by both Peter's and
Blake Edward's excesses. However, do let me have more dope
on this if you can. Best,

Letter from Satyajit Ray to D.C.R. MacDonald (Columbia UK), 9 April 1968

ARTISTS' MANAGER-AGENCY
DIRECTORS
SANFORD LIEBERSON (USA)
MANAGING
FREDDIE FIELDS (USA)
DAVID BEGELMAN (USA)
JOHN McMICHAEL
PETER RAWLEY

CREATIVE MANAGEMENT ASSOCIATES, LTD.

22 GRAFTON STREET LONDON W.1
TELEPHONE: GROSVENOR 7971   CABLES: CREMANASSO-LONDON, W.1.

April 10th, 1968.

Mr. Satyajit Ray
3 Lake Temple Road
Calcutta 29
INDIA

Dear Satyajit:

Just a note to let you know that contracts for
Peter Sellers - "The Alien"- January 1969 are
currently being drafted. While the actual signature
may take some time, I would consider this sufficient
confirmation.

Warmest regards.

Sincerely,

Sanford Lieberson

SL/mt

555 MADISON AVENUE
NEW YORK, NEW YORK 10022
MURRAY HILL 8-2020

9255 SUNSET BOULEVARD
LOS ANGELES, CALIFORNIA 90069
CRESTVIEW 3-2020

VIA LAZIO 9
ROME
480906

LICENSED ANNUALLY BY THE CITY OF WESTMINSTER

Letter from Sanford Lieberson (Creative Management Associates Ltd) to Satyajit Ray, 10 April 1968

Please note our new
telephone numbers
01-580 2090

Telephone : 01-580-1625
Telex : 263392
Cables: COLBRITPRO LDN.

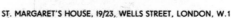

Columbia (British)
Productions Limited

ST. MARGARET'S HOUSE, 19/23, WELLS STREET, LONDON, W.1

18th April, 1968.

Mr. Satyajit Ray,
3 Lake Temple Road,
Calcutta 29,
INDIA.

Dear Satyajit,

<u>THE ALIEN</u>

    As far as the actual production is concerned, all I need
to know now is Subrata Mitra's requirements for import. We can
then get down to the completion of formalities in relation to
importing equipment and material into India, and also to making
the final schedule and budget. Have you had any thoughts on the
list of possible Devlins I sent you?

    Incidentally, THE PLANET OF THE APES with Charlton Heston
is now being shown in London. I was most impressed by the specialist
make-up by James Chambers, and feel that he might be a candidate for
creating THE ALIEN. The masks and face pieces he made to turn actors
into orangs, gorrillas and chimpanzees were brilliant. I do not know
if you will have a chance to see this yet, but please do so if a copy
is available in India. It is a 20th Century Fox film, and I think you
will enjoy it in more ways than one.

    Best wishes,

                Sincerely,

                Nick

                D.C.R. MACDONALD

cc: Mr. R. E. Atkinson   Mr. H. Court
      DIRECTORS: M. J. FRANKOVICH (U.S.A.) (CHAIRMAN)   M. SETTON (MANAGING DIRECTOR)
L. Jaffe (U.S.A.)   XXXXXXXXXX   K. L. MAIDMENT   T. L. KIRBY   A. Montague Browne

Letter from D.C.R. MacDonald (Columbia UK) to Satyajit Ray, 18 April 1968

Please note our new
Telephone number!
01-580 2090
Telephone : 01-580 4526
Telex : 263392
Cables : COLBRITPRO LDN.

Columbia (British) Productions Limited

ST. MARGARET'S HOUSE, 19/23, WELLS STREET, LONDON, W.1

18th April, 1968.

Mr. Satyajit Ray,
3 Lake Temple Road,
Calcutta 29,
<u>INDIA</u>.

Dear Satyajit,

THE ALIEN

     The newspaper cutting about THE PARTY and Peter Sellers'
antics therein could obviously be embarassing. In particular it
might provide ammunition for political sniping in your government.
It is difficult to advise from this distance, but it would seem that
two courses of action are possible for you. Either do nothing at
this stage and see what develops, or make discreet enquiries from
any of your government contacts to see if there is any possibility
of official action by them. In any case, if this type of publicity
about THE PARTY is wide spread in India, we may have to try to get
Sellers eventually to make a statement to the Indian press dissociating
himself personally from the content of the film. I realise how
sensitive this area is, but must leave the action, if any, to you at
this stage. I would have thought that the employment of any artist,
under the control of India's greatest director and performing a part
approved by the Indian authorities, should not be prejudiced by any
caricature made outside your control. Although it may be the argument
of a sophist, Sellers might be able to be presented as merely an actor
in the hands of another writer and director who should bear the major
responsibility for any bad feeling that may be created. Meanwhile, I
would suggest that you play it extremely carefully for the time being,
and if in doubt, contact me.

     I have discussed the Wilson question with Ken Maidment and our
legal department. Ken has written to Louis Blau, asking him to resolve
the situation without delay. He also suggests that you consult Blau to
confirm that you really are clear of any commitment to Indus, and that they
will have no grounds for any action against you. In relation to this, I
am enclosing a photostat of a letter which purports to sign away to Indus
the story and your services. This is something of a mystery, as we do not
know whose is the handwriting. It is not Mike's, although we do know he
was supposed to get you to sign a similar document and deliver it to us..

       cont./

DIRECTORS: M. J. FRANKOVICH (U.S.A.) (CHAIRMAN)   M. SETTON (MANAGING DIRECTOR)

L. Jaffe (U.S.A.)   ~~XXXXXXXXX~~   K. L. MAIDMENT   T. L. KIRBY   A. Montague Browne

- 2 -   18th April, 1968.

     It may be that this is merely a completed copy of an original, signed
by Mike, which we do not appear to have, but are we correct in thinking
that in any event Mike was not authorised by you to sign this letter on
your behalf? Blau should also be able to advise you regarding action
to recover the £10,000 advance on the screenplay from Mike Wilson. Mike,
in fact, drew some £22,000 from us for expenses and £16,800 producer fee
advance, so it is patently false for him to say that Columbia would not
reimburse him.

     Our only agreement at present is with Indus. If they cannot
deliver their side in terms of story, direction and music, this
agreement is obviously valueless in practical terms, whatever legal
complications may arise. Therefore, could you let us have, in so many
words, a statement to the effect that you personally own the story and
screenplay, and that you have not assigned, and do not intend to assign
to Indus the story and screenplay rights or your services as director and
composer. It may be necessary, at a later stage, to have a similar
statement formally attested.

     We urgently need to know when and where Indus was set up, who are
it's members and who has control. Could you let us have such of this
information as you possess, particularly in relation to your association
with Indus and or Michael Wilson? It might be advisable if you discuss
this also with Louis Blau before letting us have this information.

     Best wishes,

          Sincerely,

          Nick

          D.C.R. MACDONALD

Enc.

cc: Mr. M. Setton   Mr. R. E. Atkinson   Mr. T. L. Kirby
    Mr. K. L. Maidment Mr. A. E. Stroud   Mr. M. Woolne
    Mr. J. Van Eyssen   Mr. I. Tulipan   Mr. H. Court
                                   Mr. L. Blau

Letter from D.C.R. MacDonald
(Columbia UK) to Satyajit Ray,
18 April 1968

Satyajit Ray

3 Lake Temple Road, Calcutta 29   May 26,1968

Mr D C R Macdonald
Columbia British Productions Ltd
19-23 Wells Street
London W1.

Dear Nick:

Thanks for your letter of May 26. Is John Chambers a
make-up man or what? I must have more details before I
can decide what I should do about his offer.

In the last two weeks I've had a cable and a letter
from Sandy Lieberson, and a letter from Lou Blau.
Sandy says Peter is anxious to see the revised version
of the screenplay, and to know what I've done about the
ending. This last relates to a comment made by Peter to
me in Holywood about the ending not being moving enough.
He had suggested an alternative which was embarrassing in
its crude and irrelevant sentimentality. I had told him
I was convinced the ending was right and good, although
it was impossible to convey its effect in words, being
primarily a thing of sound and images. I have just written to
him personally and reiterated my views. I only hope his
raisng the subject of revision at this point is not
calculated to provide him with an excuse to quit the film.
If Peter has found about about the Indian press comments on
The Party, he might very well balk at the idea of coming out t
to work here. Hoever, I'll keep my fingers crossed, and
hope he is signed up soon.

Mike is threatening to bring a lawsuit against Colbrit,
says Blau. I must quote Blau's postscript:'If the Wilson
situation can be solved, I have no doubt The Alien can
be put together with or without Sellers.' I don't like
that 'if', and I don't like 'with or without Sellers.'
'The Alien' must be made with Sellers. If Sellers backs
out, we should think of some other story, provided
Columbia is willing to back me on a suitable alternative
project.

If we plan to start The Alien in January, I don't think
I'll do the famine story between Sptember (When I'll be
free finish the fantasy in August) and them. I'll take a
rest and then start planning for The Alien.

I'm off to Australia to attend the Sydney and Melbourne
festivals on the 29th. I'll be back on June 11, and will
be shooting in the studio right through July. This won't
get in the way of talking about the budget, should you
happen to come down within the next two months.

Have you had a chance to see my film yet? Best,

Letter from Satyajit Ray to D.C.R. MacDonald (Columbia UK), 26 May 1968

Satyajit Ray

3 Lake Temple Road, Calcutta 29   May 26, 1968

Dear Peter:

Sandy tells me that you are anxious to see the revised
version of the Alien screenplay. At the moment I have
made only 3 very small changes in accordance with the
Govt's wishes. One of these changes the name of Bajoria
to Banerja: apparently there exists a Bajoria in real
life who goes about retrieving sunken space ships in
the belief that they are temples.

There is unlikely to be any major changes in the script
but a great many embellishments by way of details, some
of which will emerge — as they always do — during shooting.
But all these refinements will have to wait until I
have finished shooting the present film at the end of
July. Since the Alien doesn't start before January, we'll
get a clear four months for preparation, orientation,
absorption etc.

As for the ending, I think I told you in Hollywood that
I thought it satisfactory. Since then I have given the
matter a great deal of thought and see no reason to
changes my views. I can assure you that it will be a
subtle, profound and deeply affecting ending. It is impossible to convey its effect in words (Haba's song, for
instance) since it'll be primarily a thing of sound
and images.

Have you seen my film The Big City? It has just opened
in London — excellent reviews — and if you should
happen to be around, you might take a look.

I hope you are having a restful holiday.

Best wishes. Yours sincerely,

Letter from Satyajit Ray to Peter Sellers, 26 May 1968

Excerpt from the SYDNEY MORNING HERALD
8 June 1968

FILM GIANT BORROWS A SUITE
CHARLES HIGHAM interviews SATYAJIT RAY, one of the great
film-makers of our day, who is now in Sydney

...What was he going to do next? *"The Alien*, a science fiction subject, with Peter Sellers." (Ray has written science fiction for children.) "It is the story of a spaceship which lands in a lotus pond in Bengal. Only the gold tip of its roof, like a spire, can be seen and the people think it's a temple. Miracles appear to take place, such as mangoes growing out of season. Bajoria, a businessman-philanthropist, to be played by Sellers, decides to salvage it, with the aid of an American engineer. The people start to pay homage when it turns out that the ship is like a living thing, with nerves and veins and what might be blood. That's all I think I should say at present."

Wasn't there a danger that Sellers might provide his usual Indian caricature? "I want him to play it quite straight. I've seen him in *The Millionairess*, and shooting *The Party*, for Blake Edwards at United Artists; he plays Indians in both. His accent at present is roughly the South Indian one, the rather 'Welsh' sound. That isn't what I need. I'll have to change him. Make his performance real."

Making it real; in those last words, the philosophy of Satyajit Ray came out loud and clear.

PETER SELLERS

37, Panton Street,
Haymarket,
London, S.W. 1.

21st June, 1968.

Sri Satyajit Ray,
3, Lake Temple Road,
Calcutta, 29,
<u>India</u>.

Dear Satyajit,

I have thought a great deal about what you
say in your letter of May 26th, and I think
I should tell you straight away that though
the part may appear more or less complete to
you, it does not seem so to me, and I don't
see how I could contemplate playing it as it
is.

However, I know you have your present picture
to finish before you can give thought to it,
and I am merely writing to tell you how I
feel and suggest that we try to solve the
problem when we meet in London in August.
I sincerely hope that we can, for I cannot
go along with the project any further while
it wears this aura of doubt.

I am sorry to say that I have not yet managed
to fit "The Big City" into my plan of action,
but am very much looking forward to seeing it
before too long.

Sincerely

Peter

Letter from Peter Sellers to Satyajit Ray, 21 June 1968

Telephone : 01-580 2090
Telex : 263392
Cables: COLBRITPRO LDN.

Columbia (British)
Productions Limited

ST. MARGARET'S HOUSE, 19/23, WELLS STREET, LONDON, W.1

11th July, 1968.

Mr. Satyajit Ray,
3 Lake Temple Road,
Calcutta 29,
<u>INDIA.</u>

Dear Satyajit,

    Since writing to you on the 4th June, we have been
in touch with New York. They, in turn, contacted Louis Blau
on June 27th. Following this I received a copy of a file note
which stated that Blau advised that we should have some word
within the next two weeks regarding a solution to the Wilson
problem. At that time, the question of the property ownership
and the assignment thereof to Columbia should also be clarified.
As far as Peter Sellers is concerned, he is part of the entire
deal, and without him Columbia would have very little interest
in the project. As you know, I am standing by to come to India,
but I have not done so yet, as it is obvious that we cannot move
any further until the situation is clarified.

    In spite of this, however, I would still like to know
Mitra's requirements. This is really extremely urgent. Assuming
everything is cleared up within the next two weeks, we still have
precious little time left for organising the import licences and
freight for those items we shall require from this country. The
non-Indian technicians and staff can also take a considerable time
to organise. Would you please hurry Mitra along?

    I saw THE PARTY the other day. While I suppose it could
be called a quite funny film on a purely mechanical slap-stick level,
I was personally appalled by the Sellers' character. It is conceived
in a completely tasteless and condescending manner, and while technically
well enough played, I found it crude vulgarity repellent. The American
reviews I have read slaughtered the picture. It has not yet been shown
here, and I find it difficult to forecast what it's reception will be.
I saw it with a group of some fifteen people, and I must admit that there
was a considerable amount of laughter around me. I am afraid that I
sat through it in appalled silence, not only because of it's tastelessness,

cont./...

DIRECTORS: L. JAFFE (U.S.A.) (CHAIRMAN) M. SETTON (MANAGING DIRECTOR)

S. SCHNEIDER (U.S.A.) K. L. MAIDMENT J. VAN EYSSEN T. L. KIRBY A. MONTAGUE BROWNE

- 2 -   11th July, 1968.

but also it's extremely old-fashioned direction and lack of shape.
Virtually, it is a collection of gags and in-jokes roughly stuck
together with little regard for tempo, and climaxing in a wildly over-
played mass scene involving the wreckage of the house where the party
is held. There are two or three excellent minor, and almost mute,
performances.

    I saw your picture a week or so ago, and was greatly impressed.
As I told you, it received excellent notices here, and I had difficulty
in getting a seat in the cinema. I thought that the wife gave a
beautiful performance and handled the development of her character most
impressively. I also found the portrayal of the stresses within the family
which I took to be a reflection of the problems caused by the increasing
urbanisation of India, both moving and revealing. The actor who played
the wife's employer also came across very strongly, and appeared an artist
of no mean ability. I have discussed the film with several people whose
opinion I respect, and they were all most complimentary. However, most
of them had one small reservation. Because of the onslaught of television
Westerners have become accustomed to rapid depiction of situation and
character. We go far less deeply into these than you do, and we tend to
rely on instant association with other situations and characters with which
we are already familiar, because we have seen their equivalents so many times
before. I suppose one could say that we are far more superficial in these
respects, but it may be a point to be borne in mind that Western audiences
are accustomed to a quicker delineation of the foundations of a film.

    I suppose I should stress that these are my personal reactions,
and are in no way official. Meanwhile, I shall await news from New York
and will contact you immediately thereupon.

    With best wishes,

Sincerely,

Nick

D.C.R. MACDONALD

Letter from D.C.R. MacDonald
(Columbia UK) to Satyajit Ray,
11 July 1968

cc: Mr. R. E. Atkinson

23 July, 68

Dear Satyajit,

I'm just back after five months in the
U.S. + U.K — have to leave again in four weeks
for the European Premiere which takes place at the big
U.N. Space Conference in Vienna. Hope to meet Dr Sarabhai
there & discuss Educational Comsats for India.

Glad to hear that you liked the movie! It's
been an exhausting experience, but worth it ... Now I
want to (a) relax (b) write short stories. But I fear
that some movie project will turn up before I can even
finish with (a).

I am sorry that there have been some
disagreements over The Alien ... hope they can be
quickly resolved. Let me know if there is any
way I can help.

all the best,

Arthur

Dear Satyajit,
    I'm just back after five months in the U.S. and U.K.—have to leave again in few weeks for the European Premiere which takes place at the big U.N. Space Conference in Vienna. Hope to meet Dr Sarabhai there & discuss Educational Comsats for India.
    Glad to hear that you liked the movie! It's been an exhausting experience, but worth it. Now I want to (a) relax (b) write short stories. But I fear that some movie project will turn up before I can even finish with (a).
    I am sorry that there have been some disagreements over The Alien... hope they can be quickly resolved. Let me know if there is any way I can help.

All the best,
Arthur

Letter from Arthur C. Clarke to Satyajit Ray, 23 July 1968

Telephone : 01-580 2090
Telex : 263392
Cables: COLBRITPRO LDN.

Columbia (British)

Productions Limited

ST. MARGARET'S HOUSE, 19/23, WELLS STREET, LONDON, W.1

8th November, 1968.

Mr. Satyajit Ray,
3 Lake Temple Road,
Calcutta 29,
<u>INDIA.</u>

Dear Satyajit,

THE ALIEN

    I have just returned from several weeks in Canada and New York, and found your letter awaiting me. The present position is that Columbia are still interested in THE ALIEN providing that

    (a) an acceptable replacement for Peter Sellers can be found and

    (b) that you are able formally to disassociate yourself from Michael Wilson so as to leave your story and services free for re-negotiations direct with us.

    I would suggest that you get Louis Blau to terminate the Indus joint venture between yourself and Wilson, so that the legal position is absolutely clear, and that you retain all the rights involved in THE ALIEN. Meanwhile, we are now in the process of examining what action we can take ourselves.

    It is obvious that this film cannot now be made in the early part of 1969, and I would therefore suggest that you start thinking of something else to do in the meantime as you state in your letter.

    I will write again more fully next week.

With best wishes,

Yours sincerely,

Nick

D.C.R. MACDONALD

DIRECTORS: L. JAFFE (U.S.A.) (CHAIRMAN) M. SETTON (MANAGING DIRECTOR)

S. SCHNEIDER (U.S.A.) K. L. MAIDMENT J. VAN EYSSEN T. L. KIRBY A. MONTAGUE BROWNE

Letter from D.C.R. MacDonald (Columbia UK) to Satyajit Ray, 8 November 1968

Columbia (British)
Productions Limited

ST. MARGARET'S HOUSE, 19/23, WELLS STREET, LONDON, W.1 P 3FP

24th July, 1969.

Mr. Satyajit Ray,
3 Lake Temple Road,
Calcutta 29,
INDIA.

Dear Satyajit,

Ismail Merchant had a meeting with John
van Eyssen two days ago, at which I was present. THE
ALIEN was the subject of the meeting.

Ismail stated that you and he had discussed
the possibility of making THE ALIEN with yourself as director
and Ismail as producer. As you know, it has always been
understood here that you function as a producer/director and
do not normally have a producer as such. I would be
grateful if you could confirm to me that you feel that you
need Ismail as producer on THE ALIEN, or indeed whether you
would want anyone at all as a producer. The reason I am
asking these questions will, I think, be obvious to you in
the light of our talk when we had lunch together recently.

Ismail is going to discuss with you the possibility
of enlarging the role of "Devlin" so that a top English speaking
star would be attracted, and whether you would want to make
THE ALIEN an Indian language film with only "Devlin" speaking
English, or whether you would shoot it almost entirely in
English. John would still prefer an English language film
at the same price as before. The fee originally planned for
Sellers would be set against that to be paid for "Devlin".

Ismail was also asked whether he and yourself would
be willing to receive no money during the next stage of script
development and writing, so that the costs could be minimal.
As you know, we have already spent a certain amount abortively

Cont./..

- 2 -   24th July, 1969.

on this subject. You will realise that, should you wish
to work with Merchant, he will require some sort of deal
for himself which will have to be absorbed within existing
budget limitations.

I look forward to hearing from you soon, and
would like to remind you that you promised to let me have
your papers concerning the earlier events regarding THE ALIEN.

Kindest personal regards,

Sincerely,

Nick

D.C.R. MACDONALD

cc: Mr. J. van Eyssen
    Mr. K. L. Maidment
    Mr. D. Niven Jr.
    Mr. P. Thompson

Cont./..

Letter from D.C.R. MacDonald
(Columbia UK) to Satyajit Ray,
24 July 1969

Excerpt from BUSINESS STANDARD
7 June 1981

Excerpts from the interview of RAY by ELA DUTTA

As skittish young college girls, we had christened him "Greek god". But youthful excesses apart, literally and metaphorically, he is a man of Olympian heights. The most compelling things about him are the radiant smile that lights up his craggy face and his rich, well-modulated bass voice. Like everything else he does, he chooses his words precisely, deliberately.

This is Satyajit Ray, 60 years old, world-famous film-maker, author, editor of children's magazine, music composer and graphic artist. He is extremely busy and also a little shy. And so he is a little chary of granting interviews.

I pinch myself when at last I am given one and am sitting in his book-lined den waiting for him to finish his work at hand. I look around while I wait. Shelves are filled with books on music, animals, reference works and a host of unusual subjects. On a southern wall hangs a beautiful old map of eastern India. A couple of porcelain dishes of lovely craftsmanship lie on the table. Casually dressed, the great director smokes a pipe. He lets down his guard after a while and answers my questions with ease and grace.

ELA DUTTA: One read in the press that you are thinking once again of making *The Alien*. Is that right?

SATYAJIT RAY: Well, there is this lawyer in San Francisco (Leonard M. Tillem). He has read the script and has been after me to do *The Alien* for a year now. He was in India recently and said that this was psychologically the right time to do it. He will produce it with another woman as a co-producer. Nothing has been signed on the dotted line yet. The script has to be redone. I thought of doing the film towards the end of the sixties and the screenplay has a flavour of that period. One has to update it and give it a certain topicality. It will be a bilingual film. At present, the mix of Bengali and English is fifty-fifty. If it is to be produced aboard then I have to introduce more English; otherwise it will need too much subtitling. Then again, after a passage of 12 years or so, a whole lot of special effects are available to us now and the script will have to be retouched to introduce these.

ELA DUTTA: Your recounting of your experience while exploring the possibilities of making *The Alien* made hilarious reading.

SATYAJIT RAY: (Laughs) One could write a whole book on all that happened. I could not put in everything in those articles. You know, I knew all along that I was being taken for a ride, but the funny thing was that the desire to experience the whole thing was also irresistible.

ELA DUTTA: What was it that made you want to do *The Alien*? Is it that you wanted to do a variety of films or was it prompted by your interest in science?

SATYAJIT RAY: I think both. Science fiction has always fascinated me. I have created the character of Professor Shonku for children's stories. At the time that I wrote *The Alien*'s script, you will recall, science fiction films were yet to come to India. *2001* and such films were still to be made. I had thought at that time of making a serious, metaphysical, science fiction film. Even today, *The Alien* will not be like the sci-fi films done in the West. There will be an element of whimsy, a certain freshness in the screenplay. And in one respect, it will be totally different. Whereas the films in the West show man's exploration of outer space, mine show extra-terrestrial beings landing on this planet. The Western films place greater importance on technology because space travel has already made great progress and everyone is familiar with the scientific principles and all the equipment involved. My film, on the other hand, will give more play to imagination and fantasy.

ELA DUTTA: If you make *The Alien*, when will you do it?

SATYAJIT RAY: Oh not yet. It is not likely to be completed before the winter of 1982.

Excerpt from THE TIMES, London
7 August 1981

SATYAJIT RAY FILM IN ENGLISH

News that the great Indian film-maker, Satyajit Ray, intends to make his first English language later this year appears to be a little premature. The film, tentatively entitled *Avatar*, is on a science fiction theme, about a spaceship which lands in a small Indian village, but Ray said in Calcutta that the project was still rather uncertain.

What he has in mind is a bilingual film, using both English and Bengali, rather along the lines of his recent success *The Chess Players*, although with rather more English dialogue.

Ray said that he would not decide on the next project until next month, but he will not be idle in the meantime; this month he starts shooting a short feature for

Indian television, a contemporary story on the issue of Untouchability, and then in winter he embarks on a major historical film, based on Rabindranath Tagore's novel, *The Home and the World*.

Excerpt from INDIA TODAY
15 February 1983

Interview of SATYAJIT RAY by SUMIT MITRA

Q. You spend a lot of time spinning fantasies yourself—in your children's literature and the fantasy films. How about a sci-fi film from you?

A. I must say it's quite impossible to make a science fantasy in this country with the kind of resources that we have here. Science fantasy is one area where Hollywood has made rapid strides. The other day, I saw a film called *Blade Runner* which is a futuristic version of Los Angeles in the year 2001. Fantastic. Quite unbelievable in technical terms.

Q. You were all set to film *The Alien*?

A. That's another story. You know, at least two of the Spielberg-Lucas films, *Close Encounters of the Third Kind* and *ET*, would not have been possible without my script of *The Alien* being available throughout America in mimeographed copies. Some days back, Arthur Clarke telephoned me from London, saying that I should file a copyright case and should not take it lying down. Other than this personal complaint, I have no quarrel with the makers of science and space fantasies. I think it's a genre full of possibilities, though I also have a feeling that Spielberg and Lucas are unnecessarily complicating the stories. The story should be simple, clear, without frills.

Excerpt from ISLAND, Colombo
20 February 1983

Satyajit Ray has had a brief encounter with Arthur Clarke—on the telephone from London. This I gather from the current issue of *India Today*. Remember *Close Encounters*?

Well, Satyajit Ray is firmly convinced that the Spielberg-Lucas films *Close Encounters of the Third Kind* and *E.T.* could "not have been possible without my script of *The Alien* being available throughout America in mimeographed copies".

Cinematic plagiarism? Violation of copyright conventions? Well, Clarke thinks so. According to Ray, Arthur Clarke urged him to "file a copyright case" and not to "take it lying down".

"I have no quarrel" says Ray "with the makers of science and space fantasies. I think it's a genre full of possibilities though I also have a feeling that Spielberg and Lucas are unnecessarily complicating the stories. The story should be simple, clear and without frills".

Excerpt from LOS ANGELES TIMES
16 March 1983

SATYAJIT RAY QUESTIONS 'E.T.' ORIGINS
DEBORAH CAULFIELD, Times Staff Writer

A 30-year veteran on the world's-best-directors list is asking some serious questions about the origins of a film by a relative newcomer—Steven Spielberg—and he's choosing to do so at a very interesting time.

Satyajit Ray, India's 62-year-old film-maker who probably is best known for The Apu trilogy, maintains that much of the storyline used in Spielberg's *E.T. The Extra-terrestrial*, a Universal release, bears strong similarity to scenes from Ray's unfilmed script *The Alien*. His script circulated through Hollywood in 1967.

Ray's statements were reported by graduate school student Aseem Chhabra in an exclusive interview for the Columbia Graduate School of Journalism's news service. Oddly, the story surfaced in the midst of the Academy of Motion Picture Arts and Sciences' annual Academy Award voting period. Neither Chhabra, nor his professor, Pete Johnson, could be reached for comment.

According to Chhabra's article, Ray said that he had approached his attorneys about suing Spielberg for plagiarism but was told that the 36-year-old film-maker "had made the necessary changes so that there is no case, there is no legal action possible in those circumstances."

Chhabra quoted remarks by Ray made on *E.T.* in the February issue of *India Today*. In the article, Ray stated that neither *E.T.* nor *Close Encounters of the Third Kind* "would have been possible without my script of *The Alien* being available throughout America in mimeographed copies." (Ray's *The Alien* is not the movie *Alien* released by 20th Century Fox in 1979.)

While Ray's allegations seem serious, given his stature, it's not the first time that someone has claimed to have cornered the market on visitors from outer space. Writer Lisa Litchfield filed a 750-million lawsuit against Spielberg shortly after *E.T.* opened, claiming that the director took the idea from her one-act play *Lokey from Maid-man*.

Writer Bam Price contacted *The Times* last summer, claiming Spielberg got the *E.T.* idea from a concept Price presented to Walt Disney many years ago. There even is talk in some quarters that the similarities between *E.T.* and an earlier draft of Columbia Pictures' *Starman* (which Spielberg saw) caused the studio to halt production on the feature until the script could be rewritten.

In all cases, the response from Spielberg has been the same—no response. When contacted for comment on the Ray allegations, personnel in Spielberg's Warner Bros. office groaned and said the director was busy packing for a overseas trip. ... While Clarke said, in an interview with Chhabra, that Ray "should write politely to Spielberg and say, 'Look—there are a lot of similarities here', but don't make any charges or threats," it seems unlikely Ray will do so.

"Sometimes I feel I ought to do something about it, but here I am in India in the middle of a film myself," Ray told Chhabra. "I can't do anything by correspondence. Besides he can deny it."

Ray added, "What he (Spielberg) has done is ruin my chance of making the film, because then people will say it came from Spielberg."

Ray told Chhabra that he was not being "vindictive". He added that Spielberg "has made good films and he is a good director".

E.T. is in Oscar competition in various categories with, among other films, Columbia Pictures' *Gandhi*, the story of India's greatest national hero.

Excerpt from LOS ANGELES TIMES
18 March 1983

PLAGIARISM TALK IRKS STUDIOS
DEBORAH CAULFIELD, Times Staff Writer

Universal Pictures is angry, Columbia Pictures is perplexed and film-maker Steven Spielberg is frustrated. All moods surfaced Wednesday in the wake of famed Indian director Satyajit Ray's allegations that Spielberg's *E.T.* contains many similarities to *The Alien*, a script Ray circulated round Hollywood in the late 1960s that was never filmed.

The story about Ray's accusations, reported in *The Times* Wednesday, was based on an article written by Aseem Chhabra. He is a student at the Columbia University Graduate School of Journalism. His story was distributed to many newspapers over the school's Columbia News Service.

In it, the Indian director claimed that his script of *The Alien* told the story of a lone alien who befriends a 10-year-old boy during a trip to the earth to study plant life. Ray said the scenes from the script—such as dead plants coming back to life around the alien—were taken directly from his story and used in *E.T.*.

The Indian director told Chhabra that he had contacted his lawyers about filing a plagiarism lawsuit against Spielberg, but was told that he had no case, since the two stories had too many differences.

Chhabra's story surfaced in the middle of final balloting for the Academy of Motion Pictures Arts and Sciences annual awards presentation. Given that Universal's *E.T.* and Columbia's *Gandhi* are top competitors, allegations were immediately flung from the upper echelons of Universal that, somehow, Columbia Pictures was behind the story. Columbia officials, on the other hand, said that they knew nothing of the story. None of the executives at either side wanted their names used.

Chhabra, contacted earlier this week, denied that the story was somehow timed to coincide with the Oscar balloting. "I read the story in the 15 Feb issue of *India Today* about Ray's feeling toward *E.T.*," Chhabra explained. "I then made all the calls to India and wrote the story." A spokesman at *India Today*'s offices in New York said that the February editon in which the article appeared went to press at the end of January. He speculated that the article was probably written sometime in late December.

Donald Johnston, a Columbia Graduate School of Journalism faculty member who is also director of the Columbia News Service, said that the story was thoroughly checked out before it ran. ...Johnston said that Chhabra's story was checked out with staff lawyers, professional editors and reviewed "line by line" to ensure that there were no statements made that were vague or that could be misconstrued. Johnston said that Chhabra tried repeatedly to contact Spielberg and his lawyer, Bruce Raimer, but that none of the calls were returned.

...A Spielberg source, who declined to be named, said the film-maker was frustrated by the latest rounds of allegations, though he declined to make any public comment.

RAY AND THE ALIEN

ASEEM CHHABRA

In 1983, I was a journalism student at Columbia University's Graduate School of Journalism, a few months away from graduating with a MS degree. I was one major project away from my graduation—to report an original news story that had not been covered by the American press. And quite by chance I stumbled upon the story about the similarities between Satyajit Ray's script *The Alien* and Steven Spielberg's critically acclaimed and box-office hit film *E.T. the Extra-Terrestrial*.

In the fall of 1982, Ray got a phone call from his friend and science fiction writer, Arthur C. Clarke. Clarke had been living permanently in Sri Lanka, but he was on a visit to London where he had seen *E.T.*.

Watching the film, Clarke was struck by the similarities between *E.T.* and *The Alien*, a script Ray had written in the mid-1960s. In Ray's script, an alien lands in a village in Bengal where he befriends a young boy. In *E.T.*, the alien lands in a small town in southern California where he becomes friends with a young boy named Elliot.

In the mid-1960s, Ray had shared the script of *The Alien* with Clarke. It was on Clarke's recommendation that Ray took his script to Hollywood in 1967 with a young producer Mike Wilson, hoping to get a studio deal to make the film. At one point, Columbia Pictures showed interest and names of top Hollywood stars including Peter Sellers, Marlon Brando and Steve McQueen were suggested for the role of an American character in Ray's film. Unfortunately, after many delays, the project was shelved and *The Alien* was never filmed.

Ray revealed the phone conversation with Clarke in an interview with *India Today* magazine in February 1983. He was asked what were his plans with the script of *The Alien*. And his response to the question was that neither *E.T.* nor Spielberg's 1977 film

Close Encounters of the Third Kind "would have been possible without my script of *The Alien* being available throughout America in mimeographed copies".

As a fan of Ray's and Spielberg's films, this interview piqued my interest. And I remembered seeing Ray's sketches of the alien in British author Marie Seton's biography *Portrait of a Director: Satyajit Ray* and how they resembled the friendly creatures that came out of the mothership towards the end of *Close Encounters*.

There was a story here to pursue, I told my professor at Columbia University. But the challenge was to talk to Clarke, Ray and perhaps also Spielberg.

So in February of 1983, I first tried to reach out to Clarke through his publisher Random House. I was asked to send the request for an interview in a letter. I pulled out my typewriter and typed a letter to Clarke, which I mailed to Random House's New York City address. I also sent a letter to Ray with a set of questions. I had managed to get his Bishop Lefroy Road address in Calcutta from a who's who sort of a book that I found in the library at the Indian Consulate in New York. And I made phone calls to Spielberg's Amblin Entertainment office in California, but had no luck in talking to the director.

While I waited patiently to hear back from Ray and Clarke, a friend at Columbia University's film school surprised me with a copy of *The Alien* script. The previous summer my friend had interned at the Merchant Ivory Productions office in Bombay where he found the script (Ray was close to Ismail Merchant and James Ivory—editing their first film *The Householder* and also composing music for *Shakespeare Wallah*). One day, he borrowed *The Alien* script, but then conveniently forgot to return it.

Reading the script, I realized that Clarke was right and indeed there were similarities between *E.T.* and *The Alien*. Ray's alien is introduced to us for the first time as we notice his slow-moving three-fingered hand, similar to E.T.'s slow-moving four-fingered hand. Ray's alien has healing powers, just like E.T.. And both the aliens could make plants bloom. There are other similarities as well.

My professor was definitely excited about the story. And naturally, there was pressure to write the story before anyone else reported it in the US.

By now, *E.T.* had become a blockbuster hit. Spielberg was a young upstart film-maker. Even though he had earlier made five important feature films, with big box-office numbers—*Sugarland Express, Jaws, Close Encounters of the Third Kind, 1941* and *Raiders of the Lost Ark*—his body of work was small in comparison to the stature Satyajit Ray had earned as one of the masters of world cinema. And my professor was aware of Ray's reputation, having followed his films—especially the Apu trilogy—during his college days.

A few weeks later, when I got no response to my letters, I took the next step. Through the local AT&T operator, I connected to the phone company's international information desk. The phone company provided this service for no extra money. I inquired if there was a listing for Arthur C. Clarke in Colombo, Sri Lanka. To my surprise, Clarke's home number was listed and one could just pick up the phone, call the number and talk to the author of *2001: A Space Odyssey*.

My interview with Clarke went well. He was warm, very approachable and friendly, especially given that I was just a journalism school student. And this is what he said to me: "I told Satyajit that he should write politely to Spielberg and say, 'Look—there are a lot of similarities here', but don't make any charges or threats." And he suggested that Spielberg had made sufficient changes to his script.

I then tried to call Marie Seton. She was a close friend of Ray and had interviewed him extensively for her book. Again, I got her number from AT&T's international desk. I remember there were five Marie Setons listed in London's phone book. And I got all five numbers. After a couple of tries, I reached the old lady who gladly agreed to give me "Showtojeet's" phone number. She spoke slowly, kept repeating herself, while I was worried the call would cost me a lot of money. And she reminded me, at least four times, to call Ray between 6 and 7 a.m., because he would always sit by his desk for that one hour.

So that is how I called Satyajit Ray from my dormitory room at Columbia University. He picked up the phone, said he had received my letter and he was going to write back. But I needed to interview him immediately since there was pressure building up from my professor. So Ray agreed to talk to me on the phone, while I recorded his voice. He told me he had not seen *E.T.*, but had talked to an attorney in Calcutta and discussed the possibility of suing Spielberg on plagiarism charges. And he told me that Columbia Pictures had circulated "dozens and dozens of copies of my script".

But Ray was also concerned that Spielberg "had made the necessary changes so that there is no case, there is no legal action possible in those circumstances". Mostly Ray sounded dejected. "Sometimes I feel I ought to do something about it, but here I am in India in the middle of a film myself (he was making *Ghare Baire* with Soumitra Chatterjee, Victor Banerjee, Swatilekha Sengupta and Jennifer Kendal Kapoor at that time)," he said to me. "I can't do anything by correspondence. Besides he (Spielberg) can deny it. What he has done is ruin my chance of making the film, because then people will say it came from Spielberg."

But then Ray added that he was not in a "vindictive" mood and that Spielberg "has made good films and he is a good director".

The story I wrote with Ray's and Clarke's voices was vetted by a couple of professors at Columbia University's law school. Then it was circulated to several newspapers by the Columbia New Service—part of the journalism school program. And the story broke out in the middle of voting for that year's Academy Awards, where *E.T.* and *Gandhi* were the frontrunners.

Some reporters wondered if I wrote the story because I was from India and I wanted *Gandhi* to win. *The Los Angeles Times* did three follow-up stories based on my article. It even quoted an unnamed spokesperson from Spielberg's office saying that the director was frustrated with Ray's allegations.

I do not think my article made the difference, but we all know that *Gandhi* swept the Oscars, winning eight trophies. *E.T.* won four awards—mostly in the technical categories, and for John Williams's score. India celebrated the recognition that was given to Richard Attenborough's *Gandhi*. Fans of *E.T.* were disappointed.

I wrote to Satyajit Ray with a set of all the clippings of my article. But he seemed disappointed and upset. He said he felt my article had earned him a reputation that he scarcely deserved. I was heartbroken.

Spielberg never openly responded to my article, but he did make peace with Ray. He along with Martin Scorsese, Ismail Merchant and James Ivory were the key filmmakers who backed Ray's honorary Oscar in 1992.

There is an interesting ending to this story. Two months after the article and the follow-up stories were published, I got a letter from Random House. The person who wrote the letter thanked me for my interest in wanting to talk to Arthur C. Clarke. But the writer added that unfortunately Clarke would not have the time to give me an interview!

ARTHUR C. CLARKE

"LESLIE'S HOUSE"

25, BARNES PLACE,   COLOMBO 7,   SRI LANKA

ආතර් සි. ක්ලාක්

"ලෙස්ලිගෙ නිවස"

25, බාස් ප ෙද ස,   කොළඹ 7,   ශ්‍ර ලංක

Satyajit Ray,
1/1, Bishop Lefroy Rd,   20 Feb 83
Calcutta 20,
INDIA

My dear Satyajit,

I'm a bit disturbed to read in today's ISLAND newspaper a report
from INDIA TODAY suggesting that I've urged you to take legal
action re. "ET's" possible plagiarism of "The Alien".

I can't remember what I actually said to you, so many months ago
- probably that after all these years (twenty, soon!) the concept
would certainly be so widely known that unconscious plagiarism
might well be possible. Also that it would be a good idea to send
a polite letter to Spielberg pointing out the similarities and
awaiting his reaction.

It is just as likely that the idea was developed completely
independently - see an amazing example of this in my preface to
Charles Sheffield's The Web Between the Worlds, enclosed.

In any event, for God's sake don't get involved with lawyers.
It's an expense of spirit (and cash) in a waste of boredom.

Incidentally I spoke to Spielberg in Los Angeles on my recent
visit - as you doubtless know, he's shooting LOST ARK II here
shortly.

Haven't seen Mike for several months, but he's still wearing
monk's robes and is in fair shape. As long as we don't meet too
often we can remain on good terms.

              All the best,

cc: Louis Blau
    Scott Meredith

Letter from Arthur C. Clarke to Satyajit Ray, 20 February 1983

A MAN WHO REVEALS TRUTH WITH DETAILS
THE TIMES Profile: Satyajit Ray by Andrew Robinson

…He has also generosity of spirit. He failed to proceed, for instance, despite the promptings of his friend Arthur C. Clarke, against the producers of *E.T.* and *Close Encounters* for lifting ideas from his screenplay for a film called *The Alien* to star Peter Sellers, which had been sent to Hollywood in 1967.
(From *The Times* London, 9 August 1984)

Telephone : 94255
Cable : UNDERSEA
COLOMBO

ಲಿಶಾಖಿ : 94255

ARTHUR C. CLARKE
"LESLIE'S HOUSE"
25, BARNES PLACE,   COLOMBO 7.   SRI LANKA

ಶ್ರೇಷ B. ಶ್ರೇಷ
"ಎಂಡಿಶಿ ಣಿಶಿ"
25,   ಶಿ ಶಿ ಶಿ   ಶಿ ಶಿ ಶಿ,   ಶಿ ಶಿ ಶಿ 7.   ಶಿ ಶಿ • ಶಿ ಶಿ

The Editor, The TIMES
200 Gray's Inn Rd.,
London. WC1X 8EZ   1984 August 14

Dear Sir,

Your profile of Satyajit Ray (August 9) states that I 'prompted' him to take action against the producers of E.T. for 'lifting ideas' from the 1967 screenplay The Alien. It is quite true that, as the initial financier of The Alien (co-authored by my then partner Mike Wilson) I wrote to Ray pointing out some striking parallels between the two screenplays, and suggesting that he contact Spielberg. My chief concern — and Ray's — was that he might be accused of plagiarism, if The Alien was ever made.

I cartainly never encouraged legal action; artists have better things to do with their time. In any case, encounters between children and friendly E.T.s are an old concept in science fiction; notable examples are Theodore Sturgeon's "Mewhu's Jet" (1946) and Robert Heinlein's novel Star Beast (1954).

When I broached the subject with Spielberg on his recent visit to Sri Lanka he replied, rather indignantly "Tell Satyajit I was a kid in High School when his script was circulating in Hollywood." I am quite happy to take his word on the matter, and would hate to cause any ill-feeling between two of the greatest geniuses the movies have ever produced.

                    Yours faithfully,

                    ath C Clab

CC: Scott Meredith
    Steven Spielberg
    Louis Blau
    SFWA; LOCUS
    (via SJ, MGM)

Dear Satyajit — F.Y.I!
Hope you're letter —
Saw Mike (aka Swami Kalki!) last
month — in f.g. shape —
all best —
                    att

Relevant portion following which Arthur C. Clarke sent a letter to the editor. *The Times,* London, 14 August 1984

APPENDIX

THE DIARY OF PROF. HESHORAM HOSHIAR: AN UNNAMED CREATURE

Sukumar Ray, Translated from the Bengali by Satyajit Ray
THE TIMES OF INDIA, 19 SEPTEMBER 1982

(Prof. Hoshiar has been very angry with us. We have, from time to time, published accounts of prehistoric animals, but never anything about the Professor's encounters with them. We admit that we have been guilty of an oversight, but the truth is, we have been wholly unaware of the Professor's exploits. However, we are very happy to publish the following extract from the Professor's diary which he has been good enough to send us. We leave it to the reader to judge the truth or otherwise of the incidents described.)

22 JUNE 1922
THE KARAKORAM. TEN MILES NORTH OF THE BANDAKUSH RANGE

Our party now consists of ten people: my nephew Chandrakhai. The two shikaris, Lakkarh and Chhakkarh Singh, six porters, and myself. Our faithful dog, too, continued to keep us company.

We pitched our tents on the bank of a river, left our baggage in the care of our porters and set out to explore, taking with us our guns, a map, and the box containing instruments and provisions.

All set for the hunt. Illustration by Sukumar Ray

Two hours of walking brought us to a strange place where everything around us seemed unfamiliar. The tall trees belonged to an unknown species. One had huge, crimson, wood-apple-like fruits hanging from the branches; another had white and yellow flowers, each over two feet long; yet another was covered with long, tapering vegetables whose pungent smell assailed our nostrils from fifty feet away.

We stood surveying this extraordinary scene when we suddenly heard loud, whooping noises from a nearby hilltop.

The two shikaris and I had our guns instantly on the ready, but Chandrakhai sat unconcerned and helped himself to jam from a couple of his tins that he had taken out of the box. This is one great failing of my nephew: proximity to food makes him oblivious of danger.

We stood thus for a minute or so when Lakkarh Singh spotted an animal slightly bigger than an elephant smiling down at him from its perch on the stout branch of a tree. For a moment, it looked like an oversized human, then it became clear that it was neither human nor simian, but a wholly new species of fauna. It sat peeling the rind of the round, crimson fruits which it ate while grinning down at us exactly like a human being. We managed to take quite a few photographs while the creature consumed fruit after fruit.

Chandrakhai now took up courage to advance towards the creature and offer it some more food. It happily gulped down a loaf of bread, a seer of molasses, and half a dozen boiled eggs with their shells which made loud cracking noises as he munched on them. It had a mind to devour the tin which contained the molasses, but after a few tentative bites it screwed up its face, broke into a whining roar and loped off into the depths of the jungle.

I have decided to name the creature Voracitherium.

A Voracitherium.
Illustration by Sukumar Ray

24 JULY 1922
TWENTY-ONE MILES NORTH OF BANDAKUSH

There is so much to see here, so many new species of flora and fauna, that much of our time is spent in finding and collecting them. We have managed to cull over 200 specimens of insects and butterflies and 500 varieties of fruits and flowers, besides taking numerous photographs. We are now looking for a live specimen of fauna to take back with us. Back home from our trip last time, nobody believed us when we described how we were set upon by a Gigantodon. A live specimen is therefore a must.

Through on oversight we had neglected to compute the height of the Bandakush peak when we climbed it. The other day, both Chandrakhai and I independently worked it out with the aid of our instrument. I arrived at 16,000 ft. and Chandrakhai at 42,000 ft. Today we took fresh measurements and it came to only two thousand and seven hundred feet. There is obviously something wrong with the instrument. But of one thing there is no doubt: this is a peak which has never been climbed before. Indeed, we are in wholly unexplored territory, with no sign of human habitation anywhere. We have to make our own maps as we go along.

There was an incident this morning. Lakkarh Singh ventured to taste a new kind

A Glumotherium.
Illustration by Sukumar Ray

of fruit which grew on a tree along our route. One bite, and he was rolling on the ground, groaning. This caused Chhakkarh to break out sobbing in a fit for commiseration for his brother. This went on for ten minutes or so after which Lakkarh Singh recovered and sat up. It was then we spotted a strange animal regarding us from behind a bush with obvious and intense disapproval. It bore the look of someone for whom the world was bereft of joy, and who had no patience whatsoever with unseemly displays of grief. I instantly decided to call it Glumotherium. I have yet to see a creature more obviously at odds with the world. We tried to mollify it with on offer of food. The beast made a grimace, then accepted half a loaf and a couple of bananas which it consumed. But then it tried some guava jelly, and this upset it so much that it smeared jelly and butter all over itself, turned its back on us and began to butt the ground with its head.

25 AUGUST 1922
25 MILES NORTH OF BANDAKUSH

This morning, we were having breakfast in the camp when we heard a funny sound coming from outside. *Tip-tap…flop-flop…tip-tap…*

We peered out and saw a strange bird hopping about in a most peculiar, zigzag fashion. It was as if the bird didn't know which way to go. If the right leg went one way, the left went the other, and if the body moved forward, the head turned towards the rear. Every dozen steps or so the legs got entangled and brought the bird down in a heap. I think its intention was to survey the camp, but as soon as it caught sight of us, it got so jumpy that it promptly fell on its face. Then it scrambled to its feet, hopped a couple of yards away on one leg, twisted its neck around and stood observing us.

"Very good," said Chandrakhai. "This is a specimen we can take back with us."

The announcement sent a ripple of excitement over the group. I turned to Chhakkarh and said, "Fire your gun. The noise will bring the bird down. Then four or five of us will go and grab it."

The moment Chhakkarh fired his rifle, the bird's knees gave away and it flopped down on the ground. Then, with its eyes fixed on us, it broke into an ear-splitting crackle accompanied by a furious flapping of wings. It was enough to put us off from approaching the bird. But Lakkarh Singh; a brave fellow, ran up and gave it a hefty thwack on the chest with his umbrella.

Up on its feet at once, the bird now grabbed Lakkarh's beard with its beak and hung on to it with claws planted on the shikari's shoulders.

Seeing his brother's plight, Chhakkarh rose to the occasion. He took a mighty swipe with his gun aiming to brain the bird. Unfortunately, he missed his mark and the butt of the rifle landed on his brother's chest. This scared the bird, causing it to release its hold on Lakkarh, who forthwith launched a fierce assault on his brother, the latter resisting with equal vigour.

A Zigzagornis.
Illustration by Sukumar Ray

For a moment, it looked as if the two would fight to death, such was the fury they displayed. Aided by two of our porters, I was trying all the while to pull Chhakkarh away from his brother. He not only resisted, but kept raining blows at his brother's nose. Chandrakhai, a portly, well-built fellow, had wound his arms around Lakkarh's waist, which didn't prevent the latter from leaping three feet into the air and whirling his rifle over his head. It just shows that the Sikhs are a race apart.

Bent on stopping the fight, we had not realized that the bird had disappeared in the meantime. However, we managed to retrieve some feathers of what I have decided to call the Zigzagornis. These, along with the photographs I have taken, ought to furnish adequate proof.

1 September 1922
On the bank of the river Kankramoti

Our provisions are fast running out. The stock of vegetables was exhausted some time ago. Now we have only some poultry left which provides us with our daily quota of eggs, some jam, biscuits, tinned milk and fruit, and some tinned meat and fish. Barely enough to last a fortnight. Which means we must be on our way back soon.

We were making an inventory of items left when Chhakkarh suddenly announced that his brother had gone out at dawn and hadn't returned yet. I told him not to worry. "Where could he have gone?" I said. "He's sure to be back soon."

But two hours passed and still no sign of Lakkarh. We were discussing whether or not to go out and look for him when we suddenly saw a very large animal looming up behind a tall, bushy tree. All we saw was its head which bobbed and swayed like a drunk's. We were about to beat a hasty retreat into our tents when we heard Lakkarh call out: "Don't run away. He's quite harmless!"

The next moment, Lakkarh emerged from behind the tree. He had the huge animal in tow, having used his turban for the purpose. He said he had gone to the river to fill his pitcher and encountered the beast on his way back. Seeing him, the animal had started to roll on the ground and make whimpering noises. Lakkarh had investigated and found a thorn in the sole of the animal's foot, and blood oozing from the wound. With

A Docilosaurus. Illustration by Sukumar Ray

great courage, Lakkarh had taken out the thorn, washed the wound and bandaged it with his handkerchief. It was when he found that the animal wouldn't be left behind, but followed him limping that Lakkarh had decided to use his turban as a leash. We all said: "Let's keep it tethered. Perhaps this is the one we can take back with us as a specimen of the Docilosaurus."

This happened in the morning. In the afternoon there was another incident. A sudden, piercing screech, like a chorus of kites and owls, was heard from near our camp. This caused the Docilosaurus, which lay on the grass feeding on the long leaves from the overhanging branch of a tree, to let out a jackal-like wail, tear itself free from its tether, and with a series of jerky hops disappear into the thickets beyond.

Dazed by the suddenness of the event, we now walked gingerly across towards the source of the shrieks, and found a large beast—a cross between a fish, a snake and a crocodile—screaming away at a tiny little creature which sat right before it with its arms and legs spread out in a gesture of utter helplessness. It seemed the big animal was about to gobble up the small one—but no: all it did was to scream at it at the top of its voice.

After about ten minutes of this Lakkarh said, "Let's put a bullet into the big one". I shook my head. "You might miss," I pointed out. "And then who knows what it might do?"

A Becharatherium and a Chillanosaurus.
Illustration by Sukumar Ray·

Our problem was solved when the beast suddenly stopped screaming and slithered off snakily towards the river. Chandrakhai said, "Let's call that a Chillanosaurus,"while Lakkarh suggested Becharatherium for the small one.

7 September 1922
On the bank of the Kankramoti
river

Making our way along the river bank, we have now reached the edge of the plateau. There is no way to proceed any further. The land in front and on two sides drops sharply down 300 feet to the plains below which have the appearance of a desert with no vegetation and no sign of life.

We stood on the steps looking down when we suddenly noticed something stirring about fifty feet below us. It was a creature the size of a smallish whale. Its head hung down like a bat's, while its tail was coiled round the stump of a tree which protruded from the cliff.

We now looked around and spotted half a dozen more such creatures. Some slept, a couple had stretched out their long necks and swung them like pendulums and one had poked its head into a crevice and appeared to be nibbling at something.

While we stood there observing the creatures, the one that we sighted first suddenly took off on its wings, swung round and came swooping down at us. We felt our limbs go numb. In our abject terror, the thought of running away didn't occur to us. In a matter of seconds, the creature was right above our heads. What followed I can only dimly recall: a most unpleasant smell, a great swirl of wings, and the terrifying metallic crackle of the creature. It was a brush from one of its wing which finally knocked me out. The others were, if anything, in a worse state than mine. When I came to and looked around, I found all my companions bleeding from wounds. One of Chhakkarh's eyes was swollen to the point which reduced it to a mere slit. Lakkarh was groaning in pain with a twisted arm. I too felt pain in my chest and back. Only Chandrakhai seemed more intent on munching biscuits held in his right hand while with the left, which held a handkerchief, he wiped off blood from his forehead and neck.

The unnamed creature. Illustration
by Sukumar Ray

We decided not to waste any more time, and set off on our journey back towards Bandakush.

(This is where the extract ends. We had written to the Professor for more details. He sent along his nephew with a note saying—"This gentleman will provide you with all additional information." Below is a verbatim account of the conversation we had with Mr Chandrakhai.)

When can we see the specimens you brought with you?

Mr C: They're all lost.

What! Lost? All those priceless specimens lost?

Mr C: We were lucky we didn't lose our lives. You have no idea about the storms in that region. One blast sent all our stuff blowing away—our tents, our baggages, our specimens, everything. Even I was blown off the ground several times. Once, I thought I was dead. The dog disappeared without a trace. You can't imagine what we went through. Maps, instruments, log books—nothing remains. You would look like porcupines with your hair standing on end if I told you how we finally got back. Struggling along without food, with nothing to guide us, it took three months to cover a distance that normally takes only a fortnight.

We take it then all the evidence has been destroyed?

Mr C: Well, I am here, my uncle is here—what more proof do you want? And here are some sketches I've brought for you. They're evidence too.

"What species of Therium are you, sir?" quipped a wag in our office.

"Bluffotherium," said another. "He just sits and spins yarns."

Visibly chafing at the remark, Mr Chandrakhai scooped up a handful of cashew nuts from a plate on our desk and strode out of the office, muttering invectives.

Translated by SATYAJIT RAY *from the Bengali story* "Heshoram Hoshiarer Diary" *written by his father,* SUKUMAR RAY. *The original story was published in* SANDESH, 1923

TIPU, THE MATHS TEACHER + THE PINK MAN

SATYAJIT RAY

TARGET MAGAZINE, AUGUST 1984

Tipu shut the geography book and glanced at the clock. He had been reading for forty-seven minutes at a stretch. Now it was thirteen minutes past three. What if he took a stroll now? It was around this time that the man had turned up the other day. He said he'd come again if Tipu had a reason to feel unhappy. Well, there was a reason now. A very good reason. What if he quietly sneaked out and took a look?

No. Mother had come out on the verandah for some reason. He heard her shooing off a crow. And then a soft, creaking noise which told him that she had set down on the armchair. Perhaps to bask in the afternoon sun. Tipu would have to wait.

He recalled the man he had met. Tipu had never seen anyone like him before. A very small man with no hair on his face, though not child. No child ever spoke in such a deep voice. Was he an old man then? Even that Tipu hadn't been able to make out. There were no wrinkles on his skin, which was pink with a touch of sandalwood yellow in it. Tipu thought of him as the Pink Man. Ha hadn't known the man's name. He had asked, but the man had said, "What's the point? You'll never be able to pronounce it without twisting your tongue."

Tipu had felt slighted and said, "Why should I twist my tongue when I can say 'indefatigability' and 'ambidextrousness' and even 'floccinacinihilipilification'?"

The man had said, "You need more than one tongue to pronounce my name."

"You mean you have more than one tongue?"

"You don't need more than one to speak Bengali."

The man was standing below the leafless shirish tree behind the house. There was an open meadow behind the shirish tree, and beyond it the paddy fields, and even further beyond was a range of low hills. A few days back, Tipu had seen a mongoose frisking around a bush close by. Today he had come with some bits of bread to

Headpiece of "Anko Sir, Golapi-babu aar Tipu" in *Sandesh*. Illustration by Satyajit Ray

scatter by the bush to tempt back the mongoose. And then he had caught sight of the strange man below the tree. Their eyes had met and the man smiled and said, "Hallo."

Was he an Englishman? Tipu was afraid the conversation wouldn't go very far if he was, so for a while he just stood saying nothing. Then the man had walked up to him and said in Bengali, "Is there anything you feel unhappy about?"

"Unhappy?"

"Unhappy."

Tipu was greatly taken aback. No one had ever asked him such a question. He had said, "Why, no, there's nothing I feel unhappy about."

"Are you sure?"

"Of course, I am sure."

"But you're supposed to feel unhappy. It showed that way in the calculations."

"What kind of calculations do you mean? I thought I'd find the mongoose, but I haven't. That makes me sorry. Is that what you mean?"

"Oh no. I mean the kind of sorrow that turns the backs of your ears green and dries up your palms."

"You mean great sorrow?"

"Yes."

"No. I have no great sorrow."

The man shook his head.

"Then there's no freedom for me yet."

"Freedom? You mean you will be free only when I have great sorrow?"

The man stared at Tipu for a while and said, "You're ten and a half years old?"

"Yes," said Tipu.

"And your name is Tarpan Choudhury?"

Ray's illustration for the story in *Sandesh*, 1982

"Yes."

"Then everything tallies."

Tipu couldn't think where the man had gathered all the information about him. He said, "It's only when I'm unhappy that you'll be free?"

"Not when you're unhappy, but when I've made you happy again."

"But so many people aren't happy," said Tipu. "Nikunja, who comes to beg and sings with his ektara says there's so one in the world to care for him. He's a very sorrowful man."

"He won't do," said the man. "Is there anyone else here who has the name and is of the same age as you?"

"Most probably not. Tarpan is not a common name."

"Then it's you I was looking for."

Tipu was puzzled by one thing and he asked, "What is this freedom you're talking about? You seem to be free enough to roam about."

"But this is not the world where I belong. I have been banished here."

"Why?"

"Why so inquisitive?"

"But I've just met you. Naturally, I want to know more about you. Where you live, what you do, what your name is..."

"To know so much may cause you jinjiria."

Actually the man hadn't said "jinjiria", but something infinitely more difficult for Tipu to pronounce. But greatly simplified, it sounded like jinjiria. Not being sure what kind of a disease jinjiria was, Tipu didn't question the man any more. Who did the man remind him of? Rumpelstiltskin? Or the little man in Ghanghasur whom Manik had met? Or one of the seven dwarfs in Snow White? Tipu adored fairy stories. His grandpa would bring three or four books of fairy stories every time he came from Calcutta during the pujas. Tipu's mind would soar across the seven seas and the thirteen rivers and the thirty-six mountains as he read them. He would be a turbaned prince, with a diamond-studded sword riding forth in quest of the string of the elephant pearls, or the fearful, fire-breathing dragon he had sworn to kill.

"Goodbye."

But the Pink Man had disappeared, having broken the world record for high jump by clearing a ten-foot-high kul tree with a leap.

All this happened a month and a half ago. The man hadn't shown up in all these days. But now he should, because Tipu was truly unhappy. And the reason for this was the new maths teacher in his school, Narahari-babu.

Tipu hadn't taken to the new teacher from the very beginning. When he came into the class the very first day, the way he stood glowering at the boys made it seem as if he wanted to turn them into ashes before he began his lesson. Tipu had never seen such a bristling moustache except on a monster in a picture book he had once read. And then the booming voice. Nobody in the class was deaf, so why bellow?

But the real trouble came two days later, on Thursday. It had been a cloudy day, which added a chill to an already cold December morning. During tiffin, Tipu stayed in the class to finish reading the story of Dalimkumar. Who would have guessed that the maths teacher would pass by the class just then?

"What's that you're reading, Tarpan?"

Tipu had to admit that the maths teacher had an excellent memory. It had taken him only two days to learn the names of all the boys in their class. Although he was a bit shaken, Tipu knew it wasn't wrong to read storybooks during recess. So he said, "It's *Thakurmar Jhuli*, sir."

"Let me see."

Tipu handed the book to the teacher. The latter leafed through it for a minute or so and said, "Ogres eating human flesh, emerald birds on diamond trees, princes hidden in sea shells—what's all this you're reading? It's nothing but fiddle-faddle. How's it going to help you in your maths?"

"But these are stories, sir," Tipu managed to say.

"Stories? Stories must make sense. You can't write poppy-cock and call them stories."

Tipu was determined not to give up so easily. He said, "But you have Hanuman and Jambuban in Ramayana, sir, and Baka the demon and Hirimba the ogress in the Mahabharata, and so much else."

"Don't be impertinent," snarled the maths teacher. "Those were written by sages two thousand years ago. Ganesh has an elephant's head on man's body, and Durga has ten arms—so what? They're not the same as your cock-and-bull stories. You should read the lives of great men, stories of travel and great discoveries, how humble men have gone up in the world through their own efforts. At your age, you should be reading real stories, true stories. These stories are for boys who walked barefoot to school, wrote on palm leaves with quills, and learnt everything by rote. Can you do all that?"

Tipu said nothing. He had no idea he'd be ticked off in such a way for reading a fairy story.

"Who else reads such books in the class?"

As a matter of fact, no one else did. Sital had once borrowed *The Folk Tales of Hindustan* from Tipu and returned it the next day saying, "Lousy stuff. Not a patch on *The Phantom*."

"Nobody else," said Tipu.

"H'm…what's your father's name?"

"Taranath Choudhury."

"Where do you live?"

"Station Road. Number 5."

"I see."

Tipu didn't go back home directly from school. Instead, he went eastwards, beyond the mango grove to Bishnuram Das's house. There, he stood leaning against a jamrul tree observing Mr Das's white horse tethered outside the house. Bishnuram-babu was the owner of a bidi factory, and rode to his office every day. Although past middle age, he was a sprightly man.

Tipu was in the habit of watching the horse, and enjoyed doing so. But today he felt gloomy. He had a feeling the maths teacher was out to stop him from reading fairy stories for good. And yet, he couldn't think of life without such stories. In a whole year, not a day has passed without his reading at least one of those stories which Narahari-babu called fiddle-faddle. And he never did badly in maths because he read such stories. Why, in the last exam he got forty-four out of fifty. And the last maths teacher, Bhudeb-babu, never said he was not well up in maths.

The days being shorter in winter, Tipu was about to make for home when something made him hide quickly behind the jamrul tree.

Narahari-babu was approaching with his books and his umbrella under his arm.

Was this the neighbourhood where he lived? Tipu wondered. There were four or five houses after Bishnuram-babu's house before the wide open stretch of Hamlatuni's field. Way back in the past, the silk factory stood in the field. The manager, for a long time, was one Mr Hamilton. He was something of a tyrant. After working for twenty years, he died in his bungalow by the factory. The local people had turned Hamilton into Hamlatuni.

In the quickly failing light of this December afternoon, Tipu watched the maths teacher from behind the tree. What he saw surprised him a great deal. The maths teacher was stroking the horse's back while making soft endearing noises.

The front door of the house now opened with a screech, and Bishnuram-babu came out with a lighted cigar in his hand.

Ray's illustration for the story in *Sandesh*, 1982

"Namaskar!"

The maths teacher had taken his hands off the horse to put his palms together and turned to Bishunram-babu. The latter returned his greeting and said, "What about a quick game?"

"That's why I've come," said Narahari-babu. So he played chess too. Tipu knew that Bishnuram-babu did. The maths teacher now said, "What a splendid horse you have! Where did you get it?"

"In Calcutta. It belonged to Mr Mitter of Sovabazar. I bought it from him. Used to be a race horse. It's called Pegasus."

Pegasus? It rang a bell in Tipu's mind, but he couldn't recall where he'd heard it.

"Pegasus?" said the maths teacher. "What an odd name!"

"But race horses do have funny names. Happy Birthday, Shobhan Allah, Forget-me-not…"

"Do you ride?"

"Oh yes. It's a fine animal. Never given me any trouble."

The maths teacher was gazing at the horse. "I used to ride regularly at one time."

"Really?"

"We lived in Sherpur then. Father was a doctor. He used to go on rounds on horseback and I would ride whenever I had a chance. But that was ages ago."

"Would you like to ride?"

"You wouldn't mind?"

"Go ahead."

Tipu watched in amazement as the maths teacher put down his books and umbrella, untied the rope and swung himself up on the back of the horse. Then, with a couple of prods on the flank with his shoes, he set the beast trotting.

"Don't go too far."

"You get the chessmen ready. I'll be back in no time."

Tipu set off homewards. It had been quite a day.

But there were more surprises in store for him…

It was a little after seven when Tipu finished his homework. He was just about to open a storybook when his father called him from downstairs.

Tipu went down to the drawing room and found the maths teacher sitting with his father. His heart stopped beating. "The books that your grandpa gave you," said his father, "Narahari-babu would like to see them."

Tipu brought the books down. Twenty-seven in all. He had to make three trips.

For ten minutes or so, the maths teacher glanced through the books. He would shake his head now and then and click his tongue. Then he put aside the books, turned to Tipu's father and said, "Listen, Mr Choudhury—what I'm going to say is the outcome of a great deal of thought on the subject. Folk tales, fairy tales and myths all do the same thing— they sow the seeds of superstition in a child's mind. Children will believe whatever they are told. Just think what a responsibility it puts on us elders. Do we tell them that the life of a human being is contained in the stomach of a boal fish when the fact is that the real place is his heart and nowhere but his heart?"

Tipu wasn't sure if his father believed all that the maths teacher was telling him, but he knew he believed in boys obeying their teachers. "When one is your age, one must learn to obey"—his father had told him many times—"especially one's elders. There is also a time when one does as one feels, but that comes when one has finished one's studies and stood on one's own legs. Then no one will tell you do this, do that. Or even if they did, you'd be free to do as you thought best. But the time for that is not now."

"Aren't there any books here suitable for one of his age?" asked the maths teacher.

"Oh yes," said Tipu's father. "Books which I won as prizes in school. Haven't you seen them, Tipu?"

"I've read them all, Father."

"All of them?"

"All of them. *The Life of Vidyasagar, The Life of Colonel Suresh Biswas, Captain Scott's Polar Expedition*, Mungo Park's *African Expedition, The Story of Steel, The Conquest of Air*…there aren't that many prizes you won, Father."

"Very well," said Father. "I'll get you some new books."

"If you place an order with Tirthankar Book Stall," said the maths teacher, "they'll get them for you from Calcutta. And those are the books you will read, Tarpan. Not these."

Not these. The two words sounded the note of doom for Tipu. *Not these.*

And to ensure that Tipu had no more access to them, Father locked them up his book case.

Mother wasn't too pleased about it, though. She kept grumbling for a while and, finally, at dinner time, she said straightaway, "What kind of a teacher is he who carries such silly notions in his head?"

Father said "no" three times in quick succession and added, "You don't understand. What he said was for Tipu's own good."

"Nonsense."

Then she put her hand on Tipu's head and said, "Don't worry; I'll tell you stories. I heard many from your grandma when I was your age. There are quite a few I remember."

Tipu said nothing. The trouble was, Tipu had already heard many stories from his mother. It was unlikely that she knew any besides the ones she'd already told. And in any case, it was much more fun reading a story from a book than listening to one. It was so wonderful to get lost in a book. How could he make Mother understand?

It took Tipu two more days to realize that he was now truly unhappy. This was the sorrow that the Pink Man was talking about. He was the only one who could do something about it.

It was Sunday. Father was taking his afternoon siesta. Ma had left the verandah and was at the sewing machine in the bedroom. It was half past three. Now was the time to go out by the back door. The man should have told him where he lived. Tipu could have gone straight to him if he didn't show up.

Tipu tiptoed down the stairs and came out by the back door.

In spite of the bright sunlight, the air was cool. The paddy fields stretched out like a carpet of gold right up to the hills. A dove kept calling mournfully, and the chirping must be coming from the squirrel that lived on the shirish tree.

"Hallo."

How strange! Tipu had no idea when the man had appeared below the tree.

"You're green behind the ears and your palms are dry, so it's clear you have cause to be unhappy."

"I certainly have."

The Pink Man moved up. He wore the same clothes as last time, and like last time the tuft of hair on his head fluttered in the breeze.

"You must tell me the cause of your sorrow, or I'd be ambifatigable."

Tipu was tickled, but he didn't bother to correct the man. He described briefly what had happened between him and the maths teacher. He was on the verge of tears as he spoke, but he checked himself with an effort.

"H'mmm…" said the Pink Man and nodded sixteen times. Tipu thought he'd never stop, and it struck him that the man was probably stumped. Tears welled up in his eyes just to think what would happen if the man let him down. But the man stopped nodding and said "hmm" again and Tipu felt relieved.

"Do you think you could help?" Tipu asked hesitantly.

"I'll have to think. I must use my stomach."

"Stomach? Don't you use your head?"

Instead of answering, the man said, "Didn't I see your maths teacher on horseback today?"

"Where? Near the Hamlatuni field?"

"Near the old broken-down factory."

"Yes, yes. Is that where you live?"

"My tridingpiditi is just behind the ruins."

That's what the strange word sounded like, although it must have been far more complicated.

The man was still there, and he had started to nod again. This time, he nodded thirty-one times. Then he stopped and said, "It's full moon tonight. If you want to see what happens, you must be there when the moon reaches the top of the date palm tree in the middle of the field. Take cover behind a bush so you're not spotted."

Tipu had a sudden frightening thought.

"I hope you're not going to kill the maths teacher?"

For the first time, the man broke into loud laughter, and Tipu saw he had two tongues in his mouth, one above the other.

"Kill him!" The man had to make a real effort to stop laughing. "No, we don't kill anybody. It was because I had the wish to pinch someone that I was banished. They decided on Earth after some calculations, and then they calculated some more and the name of this town came up. And then your name. Now I have to make you happy again so I can go home."

"Well, then—"

But the imp had once again leaped over the kul tree and vanished.

The tingling which Tipu felt in his nerves lasted till evening. What luck! Mother and Father had both been invited to dinner to Sushil-babu's for his grandson's birthday. Tipu was asked too, but the annual exams were coming up in a few days and Mother said, "You'd better stay at home and study."

They went out at seven-thirty. Tipu waited for five minutes and then, making sure that the eastern sky was touched with yellow, he sallied forth.

He took the short cut behind the school and reached Bishnuram-babu's house in ten minutes. The horse was not there. Tipu guessed it was in the stable at the back of the house. A rectangle of light from the sitting room window fell on the road. Inside the room, cigar smoke was curling up towards the ceiling.

"Check!"

That was the maths teacher playing chess with Bishnuram-babu. Wasn't he going out riding tonight? There was no way of knowing. The Pink Man had asked him to go to Hamlatuni's field. Tipu made off without a second thought.

There was the full moon, a disc of gold which would soon turn silver. It would take at least another ten minutes for it to reach the top of the date palm tree. The moonlight was soft but Tipu could make out the trees and the bushes. And the huddled ruins of the factory too. He wondered where behind it the Pink Man lived.

Tipu took cover behind a bush and prepared for the wait. He had brought a sweetmeat wrapped in a piece of newspaper in his pocket. He brought it out, took a bite off it, and chewed. The chorus of jackals sounded from the thickets in the far distance. Something dark whizzed by overhead. Must be an owl. Tipu had a deep brown shawl wrapped over his woolen jacket that would keep off the cold while keeping him hidden in the shadows.

He heard the faint sound of a clock chiming eight. Must be from Bishnuram-babu's house.

And the next moment, Tipu heard the clop-clop.

The horse was approaching. Cautiously, Tipu put out his head from behind the bush and looked intently towards the curve in the road.

Yes, there it was—the white horse with the maths teacher on its back.

But something terrible happened just then.

A mosquito had been buzzing around Tipu's head for some time, and Tipu had been trying to keep it at bay by waving his arms, but all of a sudden it found its way into his nostrils.

Tipu knew that one could keep from sneezing by pressing one's nose with one's fingers, but the thought it would trap the mosquito in his nose kept him from doing so. As a result, the inevitable sneeze came and shattered the stillness of the cold December night.

The horse stopped, and the next moment the powerful beam from a torch struck Tipu full in the face.

"Tarpan!"

Tipu felt numb. He could hardly keep on his feet. What a shame! What would the Pink Man think now that he was letting him down so badly?

The horse was trotting up towards him with the maths teacher on its back when, suddenly, it reared up, almost throwing the rider off its back, let out an ear-splitting neigh, and leaped off the road on to the field.

Ray's illustration for the story in *Sandesh*, 1982

The next moment, Tipu's eyes nearly fell out of their sockets to see that the horse was no longer on the ground. It had grown wings which it waved to lift it skywards while the maths teacher crouched down with his arms clasped tightly around its neck, the lighted torch rolling on the road where it fell from his hand.

The lower rim of the full moon now touched the tip of the date palm tree, the moonlight flooded the countryside, and Bishnuram Das's flying horse fast dwindled in size as it took its rider higher and higher in the star-filled sky.

Pegasus!

It all came back to Tipu in a flash. A Greek story. The fearsome Medusa who had venomous snakes growing on her head instead of hair, turning everyone who set eyes on her into stone, until the brave Perseus chopped her head with his sword and from her blood was born the flying horse, Pegasus.

"Go home now, Tarpan." The Pink Man stood beside him, the moonlight playing on his tuft of hair. "Everything is all right."

The maths teacher was in the hospital for three days. There were no signs of injury on his person, but he shivered from time to time and said not a word in answer to all the questions he was asked.

On the fourth day, the maths teacher came to Tipu's house. He had a talk with Tipu's father, but Tipu never found out what was said. After he left, Father called Tipu.

"You can take your books out of my book case," said Father. "He said he had no objection to your reading them."

Tipu never saw the Pink Man again. He had gone looking for him behind the tumbledown factory. On the way, he had found Bishnuram Das's horse standing as it had always done. But he found nothing behind the ruins.

Except for a small lizard, pink in colour, darting about in the rubble.

Translated by Satyajit Ray *from the Bengali story* "Anko Sir, Golapi-babu aar Tipu".
The original story was published in Sandesh Puja Annual, 1982

A NOTE ON THE SOCIETY FOR THE PRESERVATION OF SATYAJIT RAY ARCHIVES

PRESERVING A PRICELESS LEGACY

Sometime after the passing of Satyajit Ray, a number of actors and public personalities—Amitabh Bachchan and the late Ismail Merchant being among them—teamed up to form what is today the Society for the Preservation of Satyajit Ray Archives (formerly the Society for the Preservation of Satyajit Ray Films). Popularly known as Satyajit Ray Society or just Ray Society, it was founded in 1994 with the object of restoring and preserving the priceless legacies left by the master director as also disseminating his work worldwide.

RAY RESTORATION

When Ray breathed his last in 1992, negatives and prints of many of his films, especially those of his early classics, were in a precarious state. David H. Shepard, a noted film preservationist in California, came to India to examine the original negatives of the Ray films. He found the negatives of 18 of his films in 'tatters'. Restoration of Ray films was the Society's primary concern at the time. It went into a tie-up with the Los Angeles-based Academy of Motion Picture Arts and Sciences, the hallowed institution which had conferred the Oscar for Lifetime Achievement on Ray. So far, a majority of the maestro's 36-film oeuvre have been restored at the Academy Archive. More are waiting to mount the restoration anvil.

RAY ARCHIVES

Apart from his films, Ray left behind an astonishingly wide artistic universe comprising scripts, storyboards, posters, set, costume and book jacket designs, literary manuscripts, illustrations, music notations, advertisement artworks and so on. The Society has arguably the largest and most authentic archive on Ray in its custody. A veritable treasure trove, the Ray paper archive contains almost the entire creative output of his many-faceted genius. A large part of Ray's paper legacy has been restored under the supervision of Mike Wheeler, Senior Conservator (Paper Preservation) at the Victoria-Albert Museum, London, and is housed in his family home in Kolkata. The large personal library that Ray left as well as his personal effects are also being carefully preserved.

PUBLISHING RAY BOOKS

As part of its dissemination campaign, the Society has begun to publish books by and on Ray. It brought out *Deep Focus: Reflections on Cinema*, a collection of long-lost essays by Ray, in December 2011 in collaboration with HarperCollins India Publishers. In 2014, the Society published, again jointly with HarperCollins, *Satyajit Ray's Ravi Shankar*, a facsimile edition of the visual script that the master director did for his intended film on the sitar maestro. The Society brought out *Probandho Samagro*, a collection of Bengali articles by Ray, jointly with Ananda Publishers on 1 May 2015. Next, the Society brought out yet another book in collaboration with HarperCollins: *The Pather Panchali Sketchbook*, which is rich with a facsimile of the visual storyboard Ray had made for his maiden film and elaborate texts. More books are in the pipeline.

EXHIBITIONS AND FILM SHOWS

The Society has arranged quite a number of exhibitions of Ray's artworks as also festivals of his films and discussions on his work, at home and abroad. Some of the places where such shows and film retrospectives have taken place are Kolkata, Mumbai, Delhi, Toronto, Valladolid (Spain), San Francisco and London.

RAY MEMORIAL LECTURES

The Society has been organizing lectures dedicated to Ray's memory delivered by distinguished film personalities for quite a few years. Javed Akhtar gave the first lecture in 2009, followed by Shyam Benegal (in 2012) and Naseeruddin Shah (in 2014). Soumitra Chattopadhyay delivered the next lecture on the eve of Ray's 94th birth anniversary on 1 May 2015 and Aparna Sen on 1 May 2017.

www.satyajitrayworld.com

I – 12/11

ACKNOWLEDGEMENTS

Lolita Ray
Souradeep Ray
Nemai Ghosh
Debasis Mukhopadhyay
Indrani Majumdar
Pinaki De
Aseem Chhabra
Samudra Basu
Kaushik Ghosh
Udayan Mitra (HarperCollins India)
Shantanu Ray Chaudhuri (HarperCollins India)
Sohini Basak (HarperCollins India)
Joseph Antony (HarperCollins India)
Bonita Shimray (HarperCollins India)
Rajatveer Singh (HarperCollins India)
Sanjeev Kumar (HarperCollins India)
All India Radio (AIR)

We are indebted to the following newspapers and periodicals: Sight and Sound, the Statesman, the Guardian, Los Angeles Times, the New York Times, Sydney Morning Herald, the Times, London, Business Standard, India Today, the Island, the Times of India.

Satyajit Ray was a master of science fiction writing. Through his Professor Shonku stories and other fiction and non-fiction pieces, he explored the genre from various angles. In the 1960s, Ray wrote a screenplay for what would have been the first-of-its-kind sci-fi film to be made in India. It was called *The Alien* and was based on his own short story "Bonkubabur Bandhu". On being prompted by Arthur C. Clarke, who found the screenplay promising, Ray sent the script to Columbia Pictures in Hollywood, who agreed to back it, and Peter Sellers was approached to play a prominent role. Then started the "Ordeals of the Alien" as Ray calls it, as even after a series of trips to the US, UK and France, the film was never made, and more shockingly, some fifteen years later, Ray watched Steven Spielberg's film *Close Encounters of the Third Kind* and later *E.T.: The Extra-Terrestrial*, and realized these bore uncanny resemblances to his script *The Alien*, including the way the ET was designed!

A slice of hitherto undocumented cinema history, *Travails with the Alien* includes Ray's detailed essay on the project with the full script of *The Alien*, as well as the original short story on which the screenplay was based. These, presented alongside correspondence between Ray and Peter Sellers, Arthur C. Clarke, Marlon Brando, Hollywood producers who showed interest, and a fascinating essay by the young student at Columbia University's Graduate School of Journalism who broke the Spielberg story, make this book a rare and compelling read on science fiction, cinema and the art of adaptation.

Society for the Preservation
of Satyajit Ray Archives

Cover illustration **Satyajit Ray** for "Bonkubabur Bandhu" in *Sandesh*, February 1962
Courtesy **Society for the Preservation of Satyajit Ray Archives**
Cover design **Pinaki De**
www.harpercollins.co.in
f in ⓘ ⅄ HarperCollinsIN

₹ 699   ⬇ ebook
ISBN 978-93-5277-915-4

9 789352 779154   00699
CINEMA